# Agile Working and the Digital Workspace

# Agile Working and the Digital Workspace

## *Best Practices for Designing and Implementing Productivity*

John Eary

*Agile Working and the Digital Workspace: Best Practices for Designing and Implementing Productivity*



First published in 2018 by
Business Expert Press, LLC
222 East 46th Street, New York, NY 10017
www.businessexpertpress.com

ISBN-13: 978-1-94744-153-8 (paperback)
ISBN-13: 978-1-94744-154-5 (e-book)

Business Expert Press Portfolio and Project Management Collection

Collection ISSN: 2156-8189 (print)
Collection ISSN: 2156-8200 (electronic)

Cover and interior design by Exeter Premedia Services Private Ltd., Chennai, India

First edition: 2018

10 9 8 7 6 5 4 3 2 1

Printed in the United States of America.

*To my wife, Janice*

Abstract

Organizations are increasingly adopting new ways of working to take advantage of new digital technologies to enhance the services they can offer and become more productive. The aim of this book is to provide guidance on how agile working and a digital workspace can be successfully implemented in organizations that are looking to increase their productivity.

This book defines and explains the different terms that are used to describe new ways of working and identifies the benefits and limitations of different approaches. It draws on the author's extensive experience in assisting a wide range of organizations to adopt new ways of working and reflects established best practice.

You will learn about the key components of successful agile working and how a holistic approach is needed for the successful implementation of agile working. It will provide advice on the introduction of new ways of working, including preparing a robust business case, setting up an agile working program, and providing a road map. The contributions of the Internet of Things and artificial intelligence to the digital workspace and agile working are assessed.

HR, IT, property and facilities management professionals and line managers will gain an understanding of the concepts of new ways of working. They will find practical guidance in introducing agile working into their organizations and how the new initiative can be sustained.

Masters and undergraduate students in the above disciplines will gain a good grounding in the subject and they will have access to practical guidance for projects they undertake as part of their course.

Keywords

agile working, BYOD, collaborative working, digital workplace, dynamic working, flexible working, homeworking, hotdesking, mobile working, remote working, smart working, work–life balance, work–life integration

# Contents

# Foreword

The early decades of the 21st century have seen significant movement in business and social trends. On the back of new digital technology waves of opportunity have been sweeping into all sectors enabling the demolition of barriers to new ways of working. This is the age of Agile.

Agile working is increasingly viewed as a critical commercial success factor in today's digital economy. However, as Digital McKinsey reports this is not just about technology, "successful agile transformations address every aspect of the organization."

For many this means the development of new and unfamiliar operating models requiring new supporting infrastructure, skills, and settings but more importantly changes in mind-set, behaviors, and culture both within the organization and its supporting supply chain.

I have collaborated and worked with John over the last decade researching and engineering agility into a wide range of organizations. While John is a true professional, a technology project and program manager by trade, he is also an accomplished "agilista," passionate about the quest to help and support organizations on their holistic agile working change journey and successful in creating their individual agile DNA.

In the following pages John draws on this passion and the practical experience gained in "agilizing organizations" over the past two decades and his knowledge of digital working to share his insights into the successful adoption of agile working.

Paul Allsopp,
Managing Director,
The Agile Organisation

# Acknowledgments

I would like to thank Paul Allsopp for sharing his knowledge, guidance, and encouragement, Gavin Stretch for the design of the images in this book, James Eary for drawing the homeworking cartoons, Christina Jeffs and Leigh Fyffe for sharing their experiences, and Janice Eary for proof-reading and her continuous support.

# Introduction

There has been a fundamental shift in the way people work in the 21st century. The rapid development of technology such as smartphones and other mobile devices and ubiquitous connectivity mean that it is no longer necessary to be in an office to work. Already more than half (55 percent)[1] of employees work "flexibly," either on the go, at client sites, or from home. And 36 percent of employees spend at least a day a week away from the office.[2]

Offices themselves have changed to better support the various activities that people undertake in the world of work. Up to five workforce generations are at work with different expectations and experience of technology.

Management of the new workforce is challenging when employees are working remotely and often outside what are standard office hours. Today's agile workers expect more autonomy in how they choose to work and also that their well-being is considered seriously. Agile working embraces these changes. When implemented correctly it can provide increases in productivity and service provision together with significant bottom-line savings to the organization. For employees agile working offers positive improvements in the quality of their life by taking more control of their work activities. Agile working should not be restricted to management and professional staff but should offer opportunities to the whole workforce.

The digital workspace provides the technology to support agile workers. The use of communication and collaborative tools can enhance an employee's productivity. They can now have access to voice, video, messaging, and conferencing platforms from anywhere, on a range of devices. While many organizations have adopted a digital by default

---

[1] Research conducted by Davies Hickman, 2016. "The Digital Dislocation at Work." BT/Cisco.

[2] Vodafone proprietary research.

approach for their customers, they now recognize the advantages of a more digital experience for their employees.

Organizations are increasingly adopting new ways of working to take advantage of new digital technologies to enhance the services they can offer and become cost-effective. While more challenging in some sectors than others, when implemented correctly agile working and the digital workspace provide a positive employee experience, and can boost alignment, engagement, and retention.

This book aims to provide guidance on how agile working and other new ways of working can be applied effectively in organizations in the private, public, and not-for-profit sectors.

As a management consultant, I have assisted over 30 organizations in the adoption of new ways of working including major assignments in the private, public, and not-for-profit sectors. I write a regular blog on agile working, and I have contributed to seminars and webinars on the subject. I regard myself as an agile worker, and I actively practice work–life integration. Agile working has many aspects, and I have found that success is achieved by adopting a strategic, holistic approach, which I have sought to describe in this book, together with some practical insights.

Part I of this book defines the concepts underpinning agile working and distinguishes between the many different terms that have evolved enabled by developments in technology. These terms, and their features, are categorized using a ways of working progression model. The concept of the digital workspace is introduced.

Part II describes the components of agile working and how work practices can be impacted by digital approaches and introduces the concept of workstyles. The role of digital workspace and other technology components, such as collaboration tools, are discussed together with the importance of infrastructure and security. The modern workplace is described and also how it can support different types of work activities and the well-being of employees. The concept of coworking is introduced. Culture change is a critical component of the successful adoption of agile working. Ways of overcoming resistance to new ways of working and working digitally are proposed, and the concepts of work–life integration and workwrapping are introduced.

Part III describes how an organization's readiness for agile working can be assessed. The business benefits and costs that should be considered in a business case are identified, and workstyle analysis and options appraisal are explained. The formulation of an agile working strategy using a holistic approach is set out, and a road map is proposed. The governance and planning of an agile working program are described together with a list of pitfalls to avoid. The contributions of HR, IT, and facilities management to prepare and support the implementation of agile working within an organization are described.

In Part IV the critical skills required to manage agile workers are listed and the research findings on the management of agile workers with different personality types are reported. Looking to the future, the impact of artificial intelligence, the Internet of Things, and smart buildings are assessed.

# PART I

# What Is Agile Working?

While interviewing employees of large public- and private-sector organizations for a major survey on agile working, it became clear to me that many employees didn't really "get" what agile working was about. With an increasing number of organizations introducing agile working initiatives surely they will stand a higher chance of success if their employees have grasped the concept of agile working. My interviews provided evidence that most employees are familiar with flexible working, hardly surprising, as this term has been around the beginning of this century. However agile working was coined around 2008 and has not yet permeated nearly as far. Confusingly, sometimes agile working is used as a synonym for flexible working.

Furniture providers, workplace designers, and architects often describe a digital workplace as an extension of the physical workplace. But they have a vested interest as providers of furniture and physical facilities in talking about a *place* of work.

The new generations of workers are unlikely to accept the idea of working in confined physical spaces, however attractively furnished. *Digital workspaces* should support agile working to serve the needs of all employees including those who do not have ready access to desks. As Paul Allsopp, of the Agile Organisation, says "these days it's all about screens, not desks." Not every employee has a desk but most have access to a screen on at least one device. Digital work*space* rather than digital work*place* is a more appropriate description of where work activities are conducted, if currently a less common term and is used in the title of this book although the digital workplace is used in citations and other references.

With agile working there should be fewer constraints on where and when people can work with accommodation built around job tasks and technology allocated according to their job role. While more challenging in some sectors than others, when implemented correctly agile working and the digital workspace provide a positive employee experience, and can boost alignment, engagement, and retention.

# CHAPTER 1

# Defining Concepts of New Ways of Working

## Defining Agile Working and How It Is Different from Flexible Working

Flexible working is used as a general term to describe working at times and places away from the traditional full-time nine-to-five office-based employment. Flexible working has two dimensions of flexibility:

**Time,** that is, *when* employees choose to work. There are many examples of this dimension: employees can work at different times of the day (e.g., flexitime), different days of the week, (as part-time or compressed hours, job share), or specific weeks of the year (term-time working, annualized hours, etc.).

**Location**, that is, *where* employees choose to work. Again there are many examples of this dimension: in addition to the office, employees can choose to work at, or from, home, at work hubs, at cafes, while traveling.

As shown in Figure 1.1 agile working introduces a third dimension of flexibility, **autonomy**, that is, *how* people choose to work. In an organization adopting agile working employees are empowered to decide how they work to meet the goals set for them to the standards required. There may be some limitations on agile workers such as operating within the limits of their authority or competence and observing legal and regulatory requirements but they are not overly dependent on formal processes and procedures. So by this definition, a way of working that uses the same processes and practices outside of normal working hours and/or at different locations is not agile working as it lacks this third dimension called autonomy.

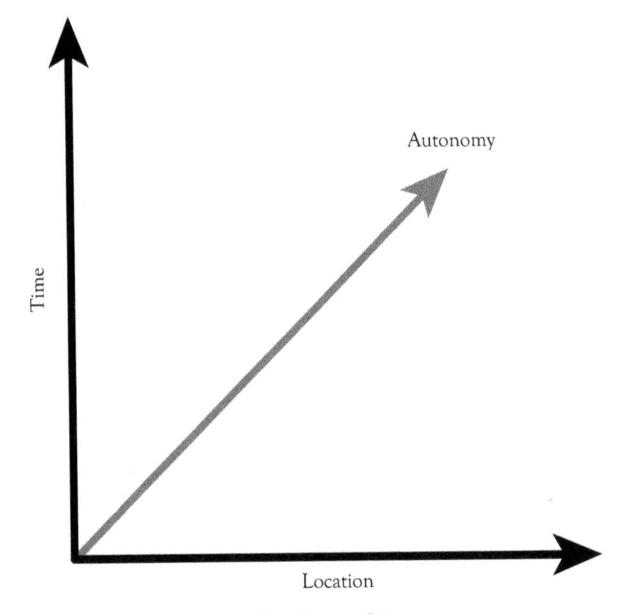

*Figure 1.1 The dimensions of agile working*

Some job roles will more readily accommodate this freedom, for example, sales roles traditionally have a significant degree of autonomy as they are set targets and are typically lightly supervised. Operational roles can be more challenging as they are often prescribed by detailed processes, and it is not impossible to introduce agile working into operational roles.

## Further Differences Between Agile Working and Flexible Working

Flexible working is generally regarded as primarily a benefit to employees. However, when implemented well agile working should provide benefits for both employers and employees. This advantage is another way of distinguishing agile working from flexible working.

> *The goals of organizations in adopting agile working are to create a more responsive, efficient, and effective organization, which improves business performance and increases customer satisfaction.*

The goals of organizations in adopting agile working are to create a more responsive, efficient, and effective organization, which improves business performance and increases customer satisfaction. By empowering their employees to work how, where, and when they choose there is evidence that they increase their productivity and provide service improvements by working in a way that suits them best. There is the very real prospect of a win-win situation. Organizations become more responsive and effective and their employees gain more control over the way they work.

Another critical difference between agile working and other forms of flexible working is commitment. While flexible working can be readily implemented with today's technology, agile working requires far more commitment from management and employees. However, the potential gains are much greater. Many flexible working initiatives have been quite small-scale with one-off savings but agile working promises transformational benefits of service improvements as well as continuing cost savings.

The Agile Organisation defines agile working as

> bringing people, processes, connectivity and technology, time and place together to find the most appropriate and effective way of working to carry out a particular task. It is working within the guidelines (of the task) but without boundaries (of how you achieve it).[1]

## How Agile Working and Agile Software Development Are Linked to Agile Organizations?

This book is about a way of working, called agile working, but agile has become an overused word. Agile can also refer to a form of software development and even more confusingly "Agile Working" is also being used in the context of software development. The UK Civil Service deliberately uses the term "Smart Working" to differentiate it from agile software development. Agile is also used as a label to describe an organization as a whole. So how do these terms link together?

---

[1] http://agile.org.uk/what-is-agile-working/

The adoption of new ways of working has given us a lexicon of terms: homeworking, mobile working, remote working, smart working, agile working, and the latest term is the digital workplace. For a definition of these terms see Appendix A: Glossary. These terms have emerged in a journey as organizations have adopted new workstyles. Each new approach has promised new benefits but often the reality of their implementation has not always provided the hoped-for gains.

There remains much confusion in the terms associated with new ways of working. It is the concepts, benefits, and requirements that these new ways of working have introduced that are important and not the labels that are often carelessly applied.

### *Agile Software Development*

Agile software development is an umbrella term for a set of methods and practices based on the values and principles expressed in the Agile Manifesto.[2]

The values are:

- **Individuals and interactions** over processes and tools
- **Working software** over comprehensive documentation
- **Customer collaboration** over contract negotiation
- **Responding to change** over following a plan

Solutions evolve through collaboration between self-organizing, cross-functional teams utilizing the appropriate practices for their context.[3]

Some of the 12 principles have a more generic application beyond software development:

[2] Beck, K., J. Grenning, R.C. Martin, M. Beedle, J. Highsmith, S. Mellor, A. van Bennekum, A. Hunt, K. Schwaber, A. Cockburn, R. Jeffries, J. Sutherland, W. Cunningham, J. Kern, D. Thomas, M. Fowler, and B. Marick. 2001. "Manifesto for Agile Software Development." http://agilemanifesto.org

[3] http://agile.org.uk/what-is-agile-working/

- No.1 Our highest priority is to satisfy the customer through the early and continuous delivery of valuable software.
- No.2 Welcome changing requirements, even late in development. Agile processes harness change for the customer's competitive advantage.
- No 5 Build projects around motivated individuals. Give them the environment and support they need, and trust them to get the job done.
- No.10 Simplicity—the art of maximizing the amount of work not done—is essential.
- No. 12 At regular intervals, the team reflects on how to become more effective, then tunes and adjusts its behavior accordingly.

Principles 5 and 10, in particular, resonate with the principles of agile working.

Agile project management is a methodology that has evolved from the agile software development approach and uses short development cycles called "sprints" to focus on continuous improvement in the development of a product or service. This approach also has more generic applications with benefits such as the more rapid deployment of solutions.

### *Agile Organizations*

Agile is a word that has no negative associations. All organizations would like to describe themselves as agile, and no organization would want to be labeled as not being agile. But what are agile organizations?

Your Dictionary[4] defines agility as "the ability to move nimbly with speed and ease." This is a definition of physical agility that could also be applied to an organization that adopts agile working, while a definition of mental agility as "flexibility of mind, a tendency to anticipate or adapt to uncertain or changing situations," could be applied to employees of agile organizations.

---

[4] http://yourdictionary.com/agility

In his paper[5] for the Royal Institution of Chartered Surveyors Paul Winter defines organizational agility as "the ability to change routines without resistance."

Goranson defined the agility of a virtual enterprise as "unplanned and unscheduled adaption to unforeseen and unexpected external circumstances."[6]

The Agile Business Consortium (formerly DSDM), with its roots in agile software development, is now focusing on business agility, which it defines as "the ability of an organization that that embraces the agile philosophy and values to:

- adapt quickly to market changes—internally and externally;
- respond rapidly and flexibly to customer demands;
- adapt and lead change in a productive and cost-effective way without compromising quality;
- continuously be at a competitive advantage."

However agile working would also claim a number of these values, for example, agile working has been defined by the Agile Organisation as "the means of empowering and supporting people to work where, when and how they choose, to maximize their productivity and deliver best value to their organization."[7] So it can be argued that both agile software development and agile working make contributions to organizations that claim to be agile.

In practice, agile organizations are free of rigid structures and sluggish decision making and are consequently leaner, more responsive, and often able to do more with less. Specifically, agile organizations claim to be:

- More creative
- More adaptive
- More responsive

[5] Paul, W. 2009. "Agile Working." *Property in the Economy.* RICS.

[6] Goranson, H.T. 1999. *The Agile Virtual Enterprise.* Westport: Quorum Books

[7] http://agile.org.uk/what-is-agile-working/

- More innovative
- More efficient
- More effective
- Less risk-averse
- Producing better outcomes

## Defining Productivity

Agile working provides opportunities to enhance employee performance and their productivity. Defining productivity is a challenge in many industry sectors. The traditional measure of productivity as the output of an employee in a specific period of time is not relevant to many job roles in today's knowledge economy. However, there are a number of components of productivity as defined in Table 1.1.

***Table 1.1 Definitions of performance measures***

| | |
|---|---|
| Efficiency | Doing more work in the same, or less, time |
| Effectiveness | Doing a better job or providing a better service |
| Timeliness | Meeting deadlines or delivering service at the right time |
| Responsiveness | Willingness to adapt to a changed requirement |
| Responsibility | Willingness to take ownership |
| Flexibility | Willingness to handle peak workload |

The quality of work, teamworking, motivation, loyalty to an employer, and job satisfaction can also be used as indirect measures of performance that can affect productivity.

In research[8] conducted for Employers Network for Equality & Inclusion (enei), factors rated as "very important" for achieving good performance by at least three quarters of agile workers across all personality types were communications, laptops, good remote access to systems and files, fast reliable networks, and calendar/diary management as shown in Figure 1.2.

[8] Eary, J. 2015. "Research Report on Agile Working, Personality & Performance." JEC Professional Services/Employers Network for Equality and Inclusion.

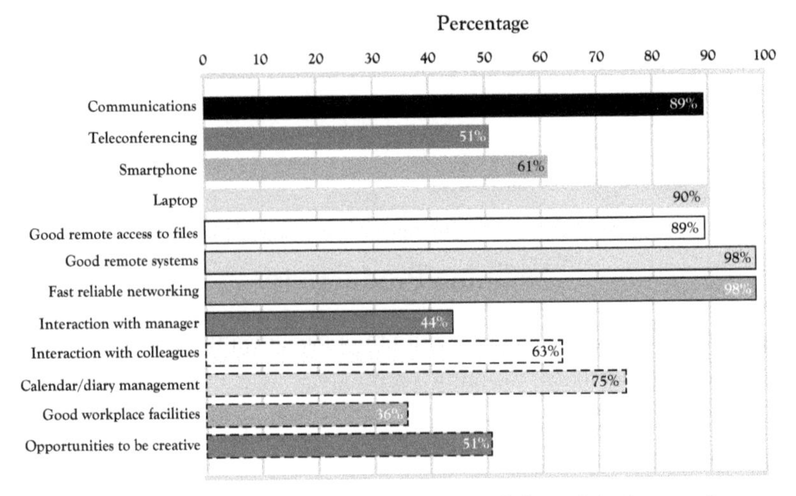


*Figure 1.2 Factors rated as "very important" for achieving good performance*

## The Ways of Working Progression Model

The ways of working progression model seeks to provide a way of assessing how organizations are progressing in the adoption of new ways of working.

The key factors are increasing choices in when, where, and how people can work. Technology has been a critical enabler for the adoption of new ways of working.

Changes in management styles and policies are required to support these new ways of working. The model shown in Figure 1.3 summarizes the development with an indication of when the ways of working were first introduced. The stages in the model also reflect a different chronology in the development of technologies that have enabled new ways of working.

### *Stage 0: Traditional Office Working*

The office has been the traditional working environment that predates the 20th century with the fixed location and time periods (as Dolly Parton sings "folks on the job from 9 to 5") for these work activities. The traditional office model offers certainty for both employers and employees.

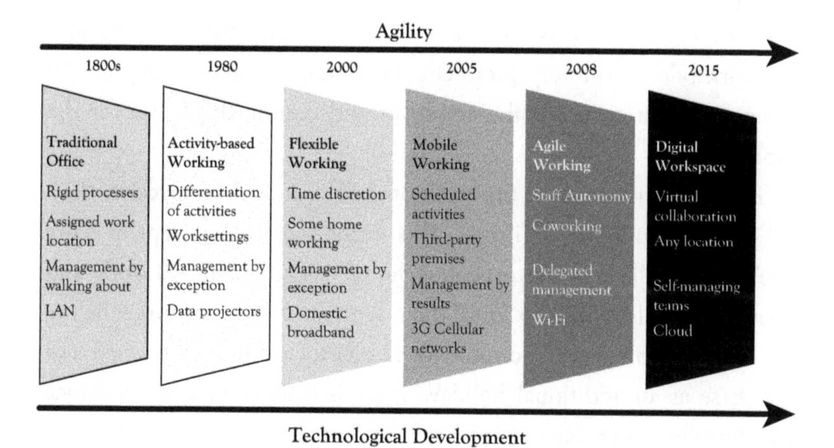


***Figure 1.3 The ways of working progression model © John Eary 2017***

In the 1960s partitions were removed to create open plan offices but work patterns remained mostly the same.

Technologies needed for the traditional office-based working are not too demanding. Typically each office worker is assigned a designated desk on which a personal computer is permanently placed connected to a local area networked to other PCs providing local access to line-of-business applications. Security is relatively straightforward as most data and systems are contained within the perimeter of the building.

Managers who like to manage by walking about can feel they are in control as their employees are under their watchful eye. Significantly the emphasis is on time spent in the office (working or not) while the quantity and quality of outputs are typically not formally measured.

Meetings can be held at short notice as employees are already on site. However to accommodate impromptu meetings, a significant part of the office accommodation needs to be dedicated to meeting rooms even if their utilization is low.

There is little incentive for process improvement as many costs are fixed. Where there is change, new processes are likely to be tightly prescribed with little scope for employee's discretion in decision making. The traditional office workstyle suits employees who find routine comforting and enjoy the daily contact and support of their colleagues.

So there's a lot to like about traditional office-based working and this workstyle is still very prevalent. However, it comes at a price, in accommodation costs for the employer and commuting costs for the employee.

The first variation from the traditional office model occurred in 1971 with the invention of flex(i)time. This introduced the concept of "core time" around which employees could choose when they started work, and when they would finish, to fulfill their contracted hours. Some schemes also enable employees to accumulate credits for extra time worked and take these as an additional holiday. There is little change in workstyle apart from managers having to accept that not all employees will be present in the office throughout the normal working day. As work activities only take place in the office, there is no need to change technology or processes. The primary requirements of this workstyle are the need for a flexitime policy so management and employees are aware of the rules of the scheme and a mechanism for recording time worked, which may be a software application or a more informal signing-in system.

### *Stage 1: Activity-Based Working*

Activity-based working has been with us since the 1980s although a number of organizations are still discovering it. It is a philosophy that aims to make work more effective and efficient, but also more enjoyable for both the organization and the employee.

The concept of activity-based working recognizes that employees need different types of work settings to accommodate the various activities they undertake in the course of a day. Rather than forcing individuals to undertake all their work at one work setting, such as a fixed desk, activity-based working provides a variety of workspaces to enable employees to conduct a range of distinct tasks in a more productive and enjoyable way. Quiet areas for reflective activities such as report writing, and stimulating places that inspire and support creative activities.

Activity-based working provides a variety of predetermined activity areas, or workspaces, to enable employees to choose the most suitable location to undertake a range of distinct tasks e.g. focused work, impromptu and informal meetings, or more formal meetings.

Office-based activity-based working makes few technological demands other than a projector or smart board to enable a participant to show a presentation or electronic document to colleagues on a screen.

Operational processes will be mostly unchanged. Management by exception may be chosen as a management style as employees are not always visible to their manager.

### *Stage 2: Flexible Working*

The first change in work location for office-based employees was allowing employees to work at home. In the UK in 2003, the Government introduced legislation that gave parents the right to request a flexible working arrangement from their employer and this right has been extended to all employees in 2014. When granted, flexible working allows employees to choose variations in when they work, for example, changes to their working day, or changes in their working week including part-time working, compressed hours (i.e., working the same hours in fewer days), and so on.

Working at home, also called telecommuting, for part of their contracted working hours, as opposed to full-time home-based working, has been a commonly requested flexible working arrangement. However, as well as these formal requests for flexible working there are often more informal arrangements between managers and employees who may bypass the HR department. There are also "Day Extenders"—managers and employees who do a "full day's work" in the office but also work at home in the evenings and/or weekends, for example, to catch up on e-mails or finish off a report.

In the UK the number of employees who say they usually work from home has increased by a fifth (19 percent) over the past decade according to an analysis published by the Trades Union Congress (TUC). The most prominent growth in regular homeworking has been among women employees, at 35 percent.[9] According to Global Workplace Analytics, in the United States regular work-at-home, among the non-self-employed population, has grown by 115 percent since 2005 and more than three

[9] https://tuc.org.uk/workplace-issues/home-working-fifth-over-last-decade-tuc-analysis-reveals

million full-time employees in the United States now work from home, up to 25 percent of the global workforce telecommutes regularly.

While partial homeworking is usually an adjunct to the traditional office routine with little perturbation to processes, homeworking has additional technology requirements. Early connections over ISDN (Integrated Services Digital Network) were often painfully slow but the increasing speed of domestic broadband has put homeworkers at a much less of a disadvantage than their office-based colleagues. And Wi-Fi has enabled devices to be used in different rooms provided health and safety considerations are met. At a minimum, all employees working at home will require an external e-mail access. Many homeworkers will need equipment to access office systems. This equipment could be a corporately owned laptop or the employee's personal PC with "thin client" software installed on it using the employee's broadband service.

Managers need to adapt their style to accommodate homeworking. They should ensure that homeworking employees are not excluded, for example, by arranging meetings at times when homeworking employees can visit the office. As with activity-based working, management by exception is often practiced.

### *Stage 3: Mobile Working*

Many employees, such as inspectors, service engineers, and sales employees, need to work "in the field," that is, making regular visits to sites away from the office.

The introduction of fast mobile data networks, 3G cellular networks from around 2005, followed by 4G networks, has been vital to the development of technology-enabled mobile working, as has been the proliferation of mobile devices—laptops, tablets and smartphones, and the upcoming wearable devices. These devices are used for e-mail and messaging and access to line-of-business applications, for applications that are feasible for mobile working.

Mobile technology allows mobile workers to keep in touch with management, colleagues, and clients. It also provides an opportunity to reduce travel time and costs through enabling mobile workers to access the information while they are "on the job" so they can go straight to their first appointment from home rather than diverting to the office. Similarly, technology can enable mobile workers to file reports remotely without returning to the office, saving further travel time and enabling greater efficiencies. These savings in time can increase productivity through additional visits and/or reduced travel as well contributing to the organization's green agenda where overall travel is reduced.

A management by results style is common, with targets such as the number of completed visits per day. However, the autonomy of mobile workers is often limited as many of these activities are scheduled for them. Mobile workers may enjoy some discretion in the decisions they make in the field.

### *Stage 4: Agile Working*

Agile working (smart working) differs from flexible working in that it is transformational, that is, based on fundamental changes in working practices, rather than incremental improvements. With agile working, performance is explicitly based on objective measures of output, and managers need to allow flexibility in how these outputs are achieved. Similarly, agile workers can choose when, and where, they carry out their work activities provided they fulfill business needs.

In flexible working (Stage 2 of the model) organizations react to employees' requests for homeworking. Agile working assumes that a proportion of the work activities will routinely be carried out away from the office. Once an organization is convinced it can continue to provide its services at appropriate and acceptable levels when employees are working away from the office, and it will encourage employees to frequently work at locations away from an office base, including coworking premises and home, where that is appropriate, for part of the working week. When employees are working in the office, they are likely to be required to work at shared desks, often called "hot desks." Hotdesking breaks the link between individual employees and designated desks and therefore increases the flexibility of accommodation. Given that fewer employees are working in the office, fewer desks and other physical facilities are needed so there is a consequential reduction in office space required. This reduced requirement can be realized as a cash benefit from the sale, or rental, of surplus accommodation. This benefit is often the key driver for many agile working initiatives.

The other benefit promised by agile working is summed up by the slogan, "work smarter not harder." To realize this benefit, existing procedures need to be challenged to identify opportunities for business process improvement. To achieve the benefits of true agile working, managers will need to engender a significant change of culture delegating some decisions and ensuring that employees can work in a more autonomous way. A light touch management style is required, based on results measured on agreed targets. Agile workers need to be empowered to make their own decisions within their competence and to react quickly and appropriately regardless of where they are situated. Agile working cannot be dictated by policy, but with education and involvement a voluntary commitment to agile working can be elicited from employees.

Connectivity is a critical technological requirement of agile working. A wireless network will free agile workers from fixed locations within their office base and enable them to work at third-party premises. There will be increased security vulnerabilities, including eavesdropping, that will need to be addressed.

### *Stage 5: Digital Workspace/Workplace*

The concept of the "Digital Workplace" is still emerging, and it is likely to continue to do so for some time. So what exactly is the digital workplace? At its least ambitious definition it is a synonym for a portal or an intranet. However Mathew W Cain of Gartner[10] describes it as "an on-going, deliberate approach to delivering a more consumer-like computing environment that is better able to facilitate innovative and flexible working practices." This definition legitimizes the digital workplace as an enabler of a new way of working. Put simply, it is a unified workplace where technology-based solutions and tools allow employees to be productive, creative, and engaged at any time, in any place.

---

10 http://thecommunicationsstrategist.com/2015/05/31/digital-communications-highlights-may-2015/

Using the preferred term "Digital Workspace" rather than "Digital Workplace," as explained in the introduction, then an effective digital workspace will have a symbiotic effect of providing an enjoyable place for employees to work while facilitating productivity gains for organizations that employ them. Digital workplaces provide employees with the freedom and flexibility to do their jobs in the best way available, wherever they are working. Furthermore as David Dunbar[11] states, "It should be a pleasant place to work, allowing people to perform at their best while maintaining the work-life balance. The Digital Workplace, like a good physical one, should be somewhere that you want to work."

Technology has evolved to support an increasingly connected digital world exploiting newly available technologies such as the Cloud. With cloud storage, files and data can be readily shared among team members, and modified using collaborative tools. For example, unified communications and collaboration services can bring together all fixed, mobile, and desktop communications services in one integrated platform that is accessible from any device. The power of today's technology means that the aspiration that people can work from anywhere, anytime can now be realized.

The digital workspace is also driving a change in the management of employees. While agile working has focused on the autonomy of the individual, the digital workspace reflects today's social media-based world and is centered on connecting people together electronically, enabling virtual collaborations between self-organizing and cross-functional teams. Management responsibility is being devolved to teams (as it is in agile software development), breaking down the hierarchies that have existed since traditional office working.

A more in-depth description of the technological aspects of digital workspace is given in Chapter 3.

[11] https://linkedin.com/pulse/unlocking-digital-workplace-david-dunbar/

# PART II

# The Components of Agile Working

There are four components of agile working as illustrated in Figure 2.1. The following four chapters describe each of these components and how they contribute to agile working and productivity.

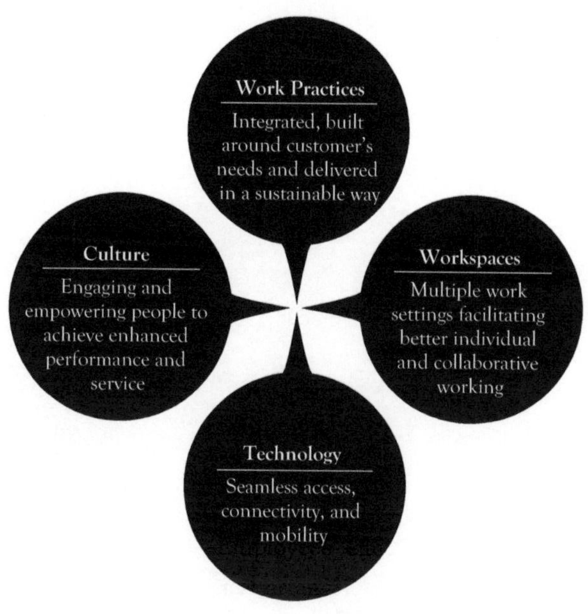


*Figure 2.1 The four components of Agile Working*

**Work Practices**—Agile working and the digital workspace are each making significant impacts on work practices and promising opportunities to increase productivity.

**Physical Workspace**—Employee's effectiveness and efficiency are impacted by the physical arrangement of the space they work in. Many employees regard their workplace as a second home, so the design of an office environment is important.

**Technology**—Technology is now more deeply entrenched in our daily lives than ever before. The rise of tablets, smartphones, and paper-thin laptops has paved the way for agile working. But technology should be treated as an enabler and not the driver for agile working. So agile working must be regarded as a business program, not a technology program. The digital workspace will significantly shape new ways of working and its effective use is the key to improvements in employee productivity.

**Culture**—Preparing for a change in culture is often the biggest challenge for organizations considering the adoption of agile working. It will require changes in management and employee attitudes and a shared vision of new ways of working.

# CHAPTER 2
# Work Practices

## Work Practices and Productivity

Before the advent of agile working, productivity was achieved by devising ever-slicker centralized processes through business process improvement. Even the bolder approach of business transformation is often a centrally imposed change. With the empowerment of agile workers productivity in the delivery of services is down to the individuals and teams working within necessary constraints and guidelines. Research conducted by Workfront[1] shows that the two most significant obstacles to work were wasteful meetings (57 percent) and excessive e-mails (53 percent).

### *Meetings*

The digital workspace has made a limited impact on meetings. Meetings are a necessary work activity in that they ensure decisions are informed and achieve consensus. While collaborative technologies have made inroads into program status and update meetings, many people feel more comfortable "pressing the flesh."

However as virtual meetings are now easy to set up and with many channels for electronic communication agile workers are at risk of spending their time in virtual meetings, taking calls, or answering e-mails, with little opportunity to reflect and decide whether these collaborative activities are improving their overall productivity. The tools that were intended to make agile workers more effective can turn out to have the adverse effect if used inappropriately.

[1] "The State of Enterprise Work" Workfront

### E-mails

E-mail is the most prevalent business communication method, and its usage is predicted to increase by a further by 4.5 percent between 2016 and 2020.[2]

Catching up on e-mails in quiet moments, outside of normal working hours, has become commonplace. It can suit employees as outstanding tasks can be quickly dealt with there and then. The working day, as far as e-mail traffic is concerned, has become stretched to cover evenings and weekends. However, extended working hours can also be a concern as discussed in Chapter 5.

The Workfront research on the use of e-mail found that most workers (55 percent) say that the main problem with e-mail is the inability to find critical information. Workfront's research indicated that the real problem was not with e-mails per se, but with the fact that 94 percent of workers used e-mail applications to manage their day-to-day work instead of using project management tools to track accountability, visibility, and work.

### Document Management

Moving paper to, and from, offices is neither desirable nor feasible. Effective agile working requires organizations to switch to readily accessible electronic documents.

While most organizations have reduced their stashes of paper documents by converting them to electronic files and forms, this is not sufficient for agile working. Many of these electronic documents are stored on shared drives, where the file structure is opaque and inconsistent making document retrieval difficult. Much unproductive time can be wasted in searching for these documents. Even worse there are still examples of documents held on personal drives that only the PC owner can access,

There is a danger of confusing ease of use with productivity. For example, editing an electronic document through word processing is faster and easier than changing a paper document. However, with this ease in amending documents we are more likely to create more versions

---

[2] The Radicati Group's E-mail Statistics Report, 2016–2020

of the document and, without the discipline of version control, there is a risk of a number of variants of the document being stored and colleagues being unclear which version is the current version.

## Workstyles

Workstyles, sometimes called work profiles, are used to describe a way of working for groups of people undertaking similar job roles.

So it should be possible to categorize the ways of working of different groups of employees in an organization by their workstyle. An accepted approach to determine workstyles is to take account of the employee's normal work locations and the degree of agility they require. There is a benefit in matching workstyles to roles, to find the optimum way of working for each role.

The following workstyles are likely to apply to a number of organizations.

- **Fixed desk** workstyle people are typically allocated the use of a desk within a single location, and all their work tasks can be located at their desk. Desks should not be "owned" by the employee and when not present for extended periods of time (e.g., more than a half day) they may be encouraged to let others use the space. While this could be regarded as a traditional workstyle, the proportion of employees in organizations that have adopted agile working is likely to be quite small.

- **Fixed location** workstyle people carry out their work tasks at a number of locations in a single building, for example, attending regular internal meetings.
- **Multi-site** workstyle people are required to work at different offices of their employer, for example, on a "campus," where offices are near to each other, or at different regional offices.
- **Nomadic** workstyle people would work across the geographical area of their responsibility, at their employer's premises and other locations (including partner premises, client premises, and home).

- **Contractual home-based** workstyle people have their home as their designated place of work, and they only visit their employer's premises for specific business reasons. Few employees choose this workstyle, which is more common for those who work freelance, or have set up their own home-based business.

Table 2.1 summarizes a number of typical workstyles that are likely to apply to a number of organizations.

*Table 2.1 Common workstyles*

| | |
|---|---|
| **Fixed desk** | Work at the same position in their base, with little or no opportunity to share space for business or occupational health reasons |
| **Fixed location** | Work in various work settings including and in a shared team area around their base |
| **Multi-site** | Work in multiple work settings around their base and also regularly at other premises owned, or leased, by their employer |
| **Nomadic** | Work the majority of their time away from a base |
| **Contractual home-based** | Contractually home-based with attendance at their employer's premises only when required for an occasional team and supervisory meetings |

Workstyle analysis is described in Chapter 7.

# CHAPTER 3

# Technologies that Support the Digital Workspace

Technology underpins the digital workspace and enables agile workers to access and share information while working in almost any location and using a variety of devices, bound only by security provisions and access rights. With cloud storage, work files, drafts, and data can be shared among team members and modified collaboratively.

The digital workspace is not a single platform or tool, such as Office 365 and other cloud-based tools, which although supporting new ways of working are not the digital workplace themselves. Similarly, the digital workspace isn't just a new name for the intranet. The digital workspace is about the combination of mobile devices, secure remote access to business information, and applications and infrastructure to support them.

The components of the digital workspace comprise:

- **Communication and collaboration tools**—including e-mail, intranets, learning management systems, chat and instant messaging apps, and collaboration tools (e.g., Slack and Microsoft Teams).
- **Content management capabilities**—including file servers and cloud-based tools such as Box and Dropbox—any cloud, or server-based, enterprise system, content management systems, internal or external websites.
- **Data and information management tools**—including databases and data warehouses, analytics tools used to produce dashboards and reports.

Deloitte[1] has a broader-based definition: "The Digital Workplace encompasses all the technologies people use to get work done in today's workplace … It ranges from your HR applications and core business applications to e-mail, instant messaging and enterprise social media tools and virtual meeting tools."

A Digital Workplace Experience survey[2] found that the most important tools in the digital workplace are:

- Document management
- Chat/collaboration
- Enterprise search
- Mobile enablement
- Unified communications

However, when asked about the effectiveness of these tools, most respondents agreed that they still need much work in optimizing the workplace.

## Empowering Employees Through the Digital Workspace

Besides saving costs and time, digital workspaces offer employees the freedom and flexibility to do their jobs in the best possible way, wherever they are working.

These new technologies can enable employees to work faster and smarter. Companies are increasingly competing on a global scale, and collaborative technologies such as videoconferencing and telepresence will be needed as the workforce is expected to function seamlessly across the world.

While technology presents very many options, it is its effective use that is paramount. Employees are empowered to do their best work when technology is supportive of their role. Ensuring that systems perform well

---

[1] https://www2.deloitte.com/content/dam/Deloitte/be/Documents/technology/The_digital_workplace_Deloitte.pdf

[2] CMS Wire/Digital Workplace Group 2017. "The 2017 State of the Digital Workplace Report." *Digital Workplace Experience.*

in remote environments is often challenging but a necessary component of successful agile working. The overuse of technology, particularly social media, can cause workplace distractions, which can hamper productivity.

The best way to encourage users to adopt and embrace a digital workspace is to address human behavior as well as technology. The digital workspace should present a pleasant environment in which to work, be easy to navigate, cater to a vast range of needs, and foster creativity. Through the collective use of connected devices, software, and interfaces digital workspace should make it effortless and natural for employees to get their work done. Intuitive, web-based access to applications, services, and content are prepared and presented to employees according to their roles. Users of digital workspaces expect fast connections, excellent performance, and reliability with the right levels of security. Increasingly employees expect to have the same service everywhere (even bandwidth-hungry services such as video).

In many organizations, employee productivity suffers because IT support services are inadequate. When digital workspaces are correctly implemented and supported, and agile workers believe technology supports their role, instead of inhibiting them, they will be empowered to do their best work. A great digital workplace ensures employees are never confused about where to go next, or where to look for information. The goal should be to make employees as enthusiastic about the tools in their digital workspace as they are with the consumer apps and devices they use in their personal life.

## Devices for Agile Working

There is a range of devices available on the market, and the selection of technology should be made on the basis of the main activities agile workers will need to undertake related to their job roles and part of a workstyle analysis. The principal categories are:

- **Smartphones** enable employees to send and reply to e-mails at any time from any location, or on the move without the need to lug a laptop around or seek out a Wi-Fi connection. Although many websites and apps are mobile-friendly, screen size is often a limiting factor with these devices, and they are not suited for roles that have tasks that require considerable data input.

- **Tablets** are often sufficient for mobile workers as they provide access to information that can be readily read on the screen and to complete electronic forms online.
- **Laptops**, particularly lightweight laptops, are often preferred by those in managerial positions and knowledge workers, as they are thought to be more appropriate than tablets for more substantial tasks, such as writing reports. For agile workers, laptops would aid productivity if they provided effective remote access to line-of-business systems. Those employees who use software applications that require considerable local computing power will prefer high-performance, often heavier, laptops.
- **Hybrid devices**, also described as two-in-one devices, or convertibles, combine the features of laptops (computing power and detachable keyboards) and tablets (light weight and long battery life). Hybrid devices can be used as a tablet in meetings, as a laptop for productive work, and as a desktop when plugged into a docking station. This versatility makes them attractive devices for many agile workers although they may be a more expensive option.
- **Desktop PCs**, multiple screens, may still be needed for employees in specific job roles (e.g., who work with larger, or multiple, documents) and can avoid the need to print out documents.

For prolonged use, laptops and tablets will need to be connected, for example, via a docking station, to a full-size screen and separate keyboards for good ergonomic and well-being reasons. The use of docking stations can be problematic if they are no longer compatible with devices that have been upgraded. The time spent trying to connect devices to docking stations is unproductive time. Several minutes wasted by agile workers each time they try to connect to a docking station will result in a considerable amount of lost time for an organization in the course of a year.

And in some cases, the frustration may deter agile workers from using shared facilities.

### *Providing Devices to Agile Workers*

Agile workers' expectations of technology have increased considerably as they travel more, spend more time out of the office with customers and clients, and expect access to data at a moment's notice. Fortunately, there is an increasing diversity of computer devices used in agile working, and it is not uncommon for employees today to use up to five devices to access corporate information. Access to the digital workspace and the user experience should, allowing for the form factor, be the same when viewed from any device. Providing a consistent experience, regardless of the device used, can maximize productivity and save time.

There are three general options for the provision of devices to employees:

1. **Get What You're Given (GWYG)**—This has been the traditional model of device provision to employees within an organization. This model is not open to any form of choice. It is therefore essential that the devices issued are appropriate to the job role of the employee. This policy can be contentious, and if the organization offers devices that are perceived as more desirable to employees according to their status, for example, managers are issued with iPads. As well as being likely to cause resentment this is not in the spirit of agile working where the device offered should be determined by the requirements of the employee's workstyle, that is, the needs of the job role and the applications the agile worker is required to use.

   For many years, many employees have felt they have better technology at home than at work. Typically, an organization will replace the device every three or four years in line with the refreshment of other IT equipment such as desktop PCs. However, employees' expectations have changed. Many employees, as consumers, now regularly replace their mobile devices annually, or at the very most every two years, in line with either their service provider's tariff or they desire a "shiny new model" that has just been released. The pace of change of new device releases means that the organizations do not have the capability, from either a resource or financial perspective, to deploy new devices to meet agile workers' desires, and this may cause some resentment. Failure to meet these expectations and employee dissatisfaction may lead to a rise in the use of unauthorized devices and applications.

2. **Choose Your Own Device (CYOD)**—allows a degree of choice for the individual, but is limited to a range of devices, typically three. Employees can decide their own trade-offs, say between the size of the screen and the weight of a laptop. By limiting the choice to one operating system, or manufacturer, the IT department is restricting the breadth of support it needs to offer.
3. **Bring Your Own Device (BYOD)**—allows employees to bring their own devices (smartphones, tablets, and laptops) and connect them to the corporate network and company services and use them for their work. (Use your own device (UYOD) would be a more appropriate term, as this would reflect the considerable numbers of agile workers who now work outside of the office.)

Employees who were provided with a GWYG device used to have their own device for personal use, but carrying around two devices, such as mobile phones, is far less common.

The use of personal devices for work purposes is now prevalent, not for underhand reasons, but it is more convenient and saves time. Increasingly employees are willing, and expecting, to use their personally owned smartphones, tablets, and other devices for work activities. Forrester Research[3] found that over half (53 percent) of employees are using their own technology for work purposes. Thirty-six percent of information workers were willing to invest their own money in a laptop, as they believed they could work more efficiently with their own kit than what they regarded as an inferior technology supplied by their employer. Seventy-four percent of IT leaders believe "BYOD can help our employees be more productive."[4]

---

[3] Q4 2011.Forrsights "Workforce Employee Survey." Forresters

[4] BYOD: Putting Users First Produces Biggest Gains, Fewest Setbacks. http// Quest.com/documents/BYOD-Putting-users-first-producers-biggest-gains-fewest-setbacks-datasheet.19142.pdf

An ISG Provider Lens™ Quadrant report,[5] focusing on digital workplace services, notes that end-user preferences, shaped by the "consumerization of IT," increasingly play a decisive role in workplace transformation initiatives. With the growing support for BYOD and a greater focus on improving user experience, enterprises are reexamining how they can empower employees via technology to increase productivity and enhance collaboration.

Employees often feel more comfortable using their own devices, especially when they are superior to the equipment provided by their employer. The agile worker may have the ability to use their personal device to access corporate systems, data, e-mail, and other services where access is secure and controllable. While agile workers may be tempted to use their personal devices, because they are to hand, agile workers' devices still need to be suited to their professional use.

*BYOD is only one part of what is called "Shadow IT," which can be defined as the unauthorized use of applications (BYOA, bring your own apps) or services that employees use without the knowledge or approval of their company's IT department. Software today is delivered via the cloud. 70 percent of Millennials admit to bringing their own apps from outside their organization to support their work.[6] Applications such as Slack, Dropbox, and Microsoft Office can be readily purchased with a credit card. A 2014 study ("The Hidden Truth Behind Shadow IT")[7] conducted by Stratecast and Frost & Sullivan found that 80 percent of employees admit to using "non-approved" applications in their daily working lives.*

Regarding support from the IT department, agile workers with CYOD devices can expect the same levels of support they would enjoy in the office although this support is unlikely to be 24/7 and geographical distance from the IT department may impact the time taken to effect physical repairs. For agile workers with BYOD devices although IT may

[5] *ISG Provider Lens™ Report* 2017. "Digital Workplace and Provider Positioning."

[6] *Tech Trends* 2015. "IT Worker of the Future—A New Breed." Deloitte University Press.

[7] The Hidden Truth Behind Shadow IT Stratecast | Frost & Sullivan 2013. http://digitaltransformation.frost.com/files/4313/9300/1515/rp-six-trends-security.pdf

offer to use their "best endeavors" there are likely to be many occasions when the agile worker is "on their own"—or seek the advice of their mobile telephony supplier.

However, IT departments increasingly expect their users of IT to be more self-reliant, for example, using online help, and are reducing the hand-holding that they use to offer, so the difference, in reality, may not be that great.

There should be a BYOD policy that sets out employees' responsibilities in the use of the organization's systems and data on their own devices and defines what support the organization can offer to employees who wish to use their personal devices for work activities.

Cost savings to the organizations from BYOD can also be significant as they do not have to procure new devices and new contracts, and the type and level of support required from IT support to the individual can, in most cases, decrease.

While it can be a significant benefit, BYOD is not practical for all organizations.

There are also some areas that need to be carefully managed and considered before full-scale organizational adoption. Managing BYOD devices is an inevitable challenge for most IT departments. Security is likely to be the greatest objection to BYOD, coupled with the complexities of personal and business data on the same device and how this will be separated and stored and transferred securely while keeping in line with new data protection rules and regulations. These points are explored later in this chapter.

As an organization, the key strategic questions when planning the adoption of, and managing, BYOD devices should be:

- What devices and operating systems will you support?
- How do you define the boundaries between personal and business usage and liability?
- Application management and governance—what applications can and cannot be accessed and how?
- Who in your business is responsible for defining and policing your mobile policy?
- Do you have the tools and resources to support a mixed-ownership estate?

## Collaborative Tools

Agile workers do not work in the same place at the same time instead they work in virtual teams, and they need online communications and collaboration tools to support them. Software tools that promote easy and seamless collaboration are a necessity for agile working and the digital workspace. As many as 65.6 percent of workers predict that, in the next two years, they will need to work more flexibly, with 53.4 percent of those anticipating that they will need better collaboration tools to do so.[8] This view is reinforced by the focus that Microsoft, Google, and Facebook have placed on developing collaboration tools in recent years. There are also more specialized "work chat" tools, such as Slack, which have grown substantially.

For voice communication, the adoption of Voice-over-Internet Protocol (VoIP), which enables people to use their computer as a telephone, and their phone number to be routed to their temporary shared desk. Also flexibility calls via VoIP can be made at a much less cost than via the public switched telephone network. Although VoIP has many supportive features to support agile working, smaller organizations may choose to equip their agile workers with mobile phones as an alternative, especially if they spend a significant portion of their time away from a base office.

Unified communications further develops VoIP by integrating voice calling with messaging and conferencing technologies, and other enterprise systems. This technology enables each employee to have a single incoming and outgoing phone number across their fixed, mobile, and desktop phone as well as one voicemail box and contact directory. This unified approach extends to collaboration tools so employees can easily share ideas through instant messaging, video conferencing, or enterprise social media tools on any device through the same unified application. A specific example is screensharing where participants in a videoconference can simultaneously see documents such as spreadsheets and presentations.

---

[8] White Paper. July 2017."Endpoint Refresh: Are you Prepared for the Future of Work?" Toshiba.

### *Making Collaboration Productive*

The digital workspace provides a whole raft of tools with the potential to improve the productivity of the agile worker through their use. However, the provision of tools does not mean that they will be used well, or even used at all. There is a danger that multiple platforms and apps can overwhelm people. Time spent on apps does not necessarily translate into real business results.

Technology has promised to deliver productivity but, in fact, productivity has not increased. A Harvard Business Review study found that, while productivity skyrocketed in the 1990s and early 2000s, it's been in decline every year since 2007. The authors suggest that, while technological breakthroughs have driven down the cost of connecting, the volume of messages makes it nearly impossible to get anything done. For example, it is estimated that over two in five (43 percent) employees use instant messaging tools at work, with Skype (29 percent), Facebook Messenger (22 percent), Lync (19 percent), and Slack (5 percent) making up the top four.[9] This confusion can impact productivity and employee engagement.

All respondents felt that the tools they had access to were too specific to be used effectively. Nearly half (46 percent) of the respondents from the Harvard survey said that they were unable to connect collaborators from outside the organization with those inside because of concerns about privacy, security, and access management.[10]

The digital workspace is far from stable. A digital workplace platform should be able to accommodate solutions that already work well. Furthermore, with the growing number of collaboration and communication solutions available within an organization, information can become scattered across many systems—making it increasingly difficult to monitor and manage solutions and protect the organization's data.

The proliferation of digital tools can be confusing, and people will be reluctant to learn to use one tool if they feel it is likely to be replaced by another in a short period of time. It is essential to test and decide which tools are effective for the organization's agile workers, and then provide

---

[9] 2017. http://hrdive.com/news/poll-43-of-employees-use-instant-messaging-tools-on-the-job/444599/

[10] "Analytic Services Survey. August 2016." *Harvard Business Review.*

learning on these specific tools to ensure they are being used effectively. Some organizations may choose to meet the needs of older generations in the workforce who prefer interfacing with existing software and tools.

### *The Appropriateness of Communication Tools*

There are workplace tools accessible from a range of devices for task management, chat, videoconferencing, and a wide range of other functions, which are intended to help people work better together. Recognizing the suitability of different collaboration tools is essential. For example, the quality of your communications is important. Different media are better suited for different situations. Table 3.1 proposes a hierarchy of communication power.

*Table 3.1 Hierarchy of communication tools*

| Hierarchy | Communication tool | Pros | Cons |
|---|---|---|---|
| 1 | Videoconference | • Highly engaging<br>• Communicates body language<br>• Suited for sensitive or complicated issues<br>• Can reduce misunderstandings by providing visual cues<br>• Plays a supporting role for remote workers<br>• Webcams on portable devices enable face-to-face communication regardless of location | • Can take more time to arrange as participants need to be in suitable locations<br>• Employees may feel uncomfortable<br>• Needs to be held in real time |
| 2 | Audioconference | • Quick to set up and can be held at short notice<br>• Can convey subtlety through tone of voice | • Needs to be held in real time<br>• Participants may find it hard to stay focused on longer calls |

(*Continued*)

*Table 3.1 (Continued)*

| Hierarchy | Communication tool | Pros | Cons |
|---|---|---|---|
| | | • Suited for routine report back meetings<br>• Quicker to convey information than writing<br>• Suited for discussion<br>• Will become cheaper with WebRTC (real-time communication)<br>• Optionally documents can be shared | • Participants can be distracted during the call, for example, by receiving e-mails |
| 3 | Chat | • Suited for informal messaging<br>• Good for quick questions and focused conversations between colleagues<br>• Suited for daily updates<br>• Doesn't clutter people's inboxes. | • Not suited for resolving issues or disagreements<br>• No automatic record keeping |
| 4 | E-mail | • Good for formal communication<br>• Good for detailed communication | • Can be misinterpreted |

Videoconferencing is now a more feasible alternative to in-person meetings, thanks to both faster and more reliable Internet speeds and improved technologies. Having the ability to get face-to-face with colleagues without being in the same physical space is another important collaboration tool—three-quarters of senior management believe that videoconferencing will replace conference calls and become the preferred method of business communication in the future.[11] However physical

[11] https://powwownow.co.uk/smarter-working/rise-video-conferencing

face-to-face meetings are still required for situations such as disciplinary matters. Visual cues can play a significant role in effective communication. When using videoconferencing even small details need attention. For example, participants may be put off if facial expressions are hidden in shadow because participants are are not well lit. In summary, collaboration needs to be carefully designed. Ideally, the digital workspace provides a unified access point for the tools they need. Ultimately, it has to facilitate the best ways to bring agile workers together and increase their connectedness and productivity as a result. If not, it will quickly be sidelined. Staff will find other tools to use instead. An effective digital workspace will make it seamless and straightforward to work together regardless of distance.

## Providing an Infrastructure to Support Agile Working

While the alluring variety of mobile devices grabs the agile working technology headlines more important is how these devices are connected to corporate information systems. To underpin the effective use of technology organizations need to have the infrastructure in place to provide easy, fast, and secure access to corporate networks, and the systems that employees need to work effectively.

There is a range of ways to provide IT infrastructure to support agile working, but there are two key building blocks:

1. The "service" through which the application software is provided
2. A "connection"—which can include 3G or 4G networks, public and private Wi-Fi

### *Providing the Service*

For a computing device to be useful to an agile worker, it needs to connect to services. A service could be as simple as a web page on the Internet, or as complicated as a control system for a proprietary piece of equipment connected to an internal network behind a firewall.

Other examples of services could include:

- Company intranet
- Access to e-mails
- Access to files and folders
- Telephony and communication/collaboration tools
- CRM (customer relationship management) systems
- ERP (enterprise resource planning) systems

There are five main ways of providing a service to support agile working:

**Web-based utility software**. The service requirements of some agile workers are quite limited. Basic services such as e-mail, contacts, and calendars are common to all users but are especially important to agile workers. The traditional corporate Exchange server provision is being supplemented, or replaced by web e-mail such as Gmail or Office 365 where a wide variety of devices need to be supported.

With a **hosted or virtual corporate desktop**, the agile worker can access their desktop through their device, using software such as Quest, Citrix, or VMware. The appropriate client software or web browser is installed on the device. This solution is mostly device independent, so will work with everything from a tablet to a smartphone. It will need appropriate back-end support and processing and means that the user cannot work on corporate applications unless they are authorized to be connected to the network.

A **client hypervisor** with desktop check-in/check-out software on the device is a particularly useful solution for agile workers who need to use laptops. However, this places higher demands on the IT team, as they need to configure the user device and install the client hypervisor to accept the virtual desktop. It works by partitioning the hard drive into business and personal areas and can then be run locally. If a user goes online, it checks back into the server. However, it is not possible to run a full corporate desktop on devices such as tablets or BYOD devices.

In a **portal-based** approach, applications can be accessed through a portal (similar to iTunes). This approach requires either application streaming, or the creation of lightweight clients that can run on a smartphone or tablet, to run basic functions, while most of the processing is carried out remotely. However, this approach is not suitable for "large" applications.

**Hosted or cloud-based** solutions, such as Google Docs and Microsoft Office 365, are available for organizations that do not want the servers, IT employees, or the overhead of managing internal solutions. If the solution is bought as a service, payment is simply per user, per month, and charges can increase or decrease in line with the number of users.

### *Managing the Connection*

For agile workers' peripatetic workstyle wireless, in addition to wired connections, is needed, and the choice is either Wi-Fi or mobile telephony.

Wi-Fi can be provided in three main ways:

1. **Corporately** in the offices that are used by agile workers, including satellite offices. Some organizations offer public Wi-Fi access for visitors, which can also be used by agile workers with BYOD devices.
2. **Publicly** through hotspot service at coffee shops and hotels, for example, by BT Openzone or The Cloud—however, these are often regarded as insecure.
3. **Privately**, for example, through agile workers' residential broadband when working at home.

Mobile telephony readily meets the "anyplace, anywhere" requirements of agile working. For most agile workers Wi-Fi rarely matches this level of accessibility although Wi-Fi is usually a cheaper solution than mobile telephony.

The speed of mobile telephony has progressed from GPRS (General Packet Radio Services), EDGE (Enhanced Data GSM Environment), and 3G to the high-speed 4G (fourth-generation mobile networks) and forthcoming 5G. In fact, 4G mobile networks have the ability to offer download speeds of up to 80Mb compared to 50Mb typical of "high-speed" home broadband. 4G could enable some agile workers to obtain a faster Internet connection when stood in the street with a mobile device, than when sat at a computer in their home or an office, albeit at a cost.

The performance of the network connection is vital to agile workers and their (often high) expectation that they will enjoy the same service outside the office as inside the office. The performance of Internet connections is affected by two factors:

- Network speed, or "bandwidth," which indicates how fast data moves between two points
- Network delay, or "latency," which indicates how long it takes for each request for the data to travel between two points or two computers

It is entirely possible to have a large amount of bandwidth on an Internet connection, but still get a poor quality service or experience if there is a significant amount of "latency" on the connection, for example, accessing applications, on a high latency network, the display and screen updates will be very slow. If the mobile device is carrying out a lot of tasks "locally" then performance could be impacted by low bandwidth.

## Addressing the Security Issues of Agile Working

An essential requirement of agile working is that information can be accessed at any time by people authorized to see it. However, this information needs to be protected from loss or theft and can be stored, archived, and deleted safely and securely. Agile workers working in multiple locations undoubtedly add to the risks of loss of data and privacy issues, for example, through the loss of mobile devices and paper documents. If agile workers lose their device, they may not be contactable and may not be able to see their e-mails. The loss of the device can also pose significant security risks.

A particular concern is data; while much of the data is now held on corporate servers a significant amount of business data, often sensitive in nature, could be stored on mobile devices, where corporate and private data may coexist for employees adopting a work–life integration workstyle. An organization could lose sight and control of its data if it is only stored on an employee's personal device. If data is not stored on the corporate network, at best it will be backed up through the agile worker's personal backup facilities, and at worst it will not be backed up at all.

Corporate data could also be at risk from unauthorized access through mobile devices. This can be a very serious concern if the device contains data that is commercially sensitive or contains personal details. As more organizations connect to the Cloud, security concerns shift to issues around identity. It is vital that users' corporate identities can be verified, entirely securely, to give them access to the applications and data they need. A serious security breach by an agile worker, as well as causing embarrassment for the employee and employing organization, is also likely to set back the cause of agile working.

A number of surveys have highlighted security threats as being one of the greatest concerns for businesses adopting agile working especially those using personal devices.

- A 2013 survey, commissioned by the ICO (The UK's Information Commissioner's Office) and carried out by YouGov, revealed that 47 percent of all UK adults now use their personal smartphone, laptop, or tablet computer for work purposes. But fewer than 3 in 10 who do so are provided with guidance on how their devices should be used in this capacity.
- 66 percent of employees admitted that they regularly e-mail company files to personal e-mail addresses so they can work from home in a research conducted by Pierre Audoin Consultants.[12]

Audoin's research also shows that technology is seen as a barrier rather than an enabler for workplace changes.

Among the key findings was the fact that security is increasingly seen to be holding back productivity in the workplace. Businesses

[12] Vodafone Ready Business Test Results 2015.

are struggling to effectively address the constant threat of cybercrime while also providing the tools and environment needed for effective internal and external collaboration.

Companies have responded to the security threat by investing heavily in cyber defense, but for many of them this is having an adverse effect on productivity. There is some evidence that workplace security is having an adverse effect on employee productivity. In a survey[13] by Pierre Audoin Consultants more than half of the study participants (56 percent) believe their current approach to workplace security has a negative impact, with 20 percent saying it has a "highly negative" effect. This view is often caused by employees taking noncompliant routes and cutting corners when faced with complicated or time-consuming security procedures and mechanisms. Security is also preventing businesses from taking full advantage of collaboration-based tools. According to the study, 41 percent of businesses have not yet deployed these tools with 46 percent naming security concerns as the principal barrier. The digital workspace needs to set out to balance freedom of choice in the productive use of technology with security, ensuring secure, remote access to business information and applications.

### *Mitigating Data Loss from Agile Working*

It is essential that the security risks of agile working are addressed. Fortunately, there is a range of powerful security tools to ensure the safety and security of data in the digital workspace such as:

- **Encryption**—which protects information by scrambling the original message with a very long digital key. The computer receiving the message knows the key and so is able to decrypt the original message. As long as the secret key is only known by trusted parties, the cipher-text is very hard to de-crypt or un-encrypt by external parties. Having encryption enabled means that, if an agile worker loses a mobile device, it is

[13] Pierre Audoin Consultants. 2017. "Digital Workplace in Europe"

highly unlikely that anyone who finds it can get any information from it. Where encryption is not feasible, an organization may determine that specific applications such as those involving legal records will not be used over noncorporate connections.

- **Authentication**—is a way of ensuring that somebody is who they say they are. Typically it is a combination of something the agile worker knows (such as a password or PIN code), something the agile worker has (such as a security device, or token), or a personal attribute concerning the agile worker (technology that makes use of fingerprint recognition, retina scans, or facial recognition). With these authentication factors remotely held data cannot be accessed from lost or stolen devices. Smartphone apps have been developed, such as HP WorkWise, which unlocks the PC as the employee approaches it and automatically locks the device as the employee walks away.
- **Remote wipe**—is a feature that allows IT support teams to remotely delete all information held on a device if the agile worker has reported the device as lost or stolen. For many organizations, having data stored locally on a device is only acceptable if that device has a remote wipe capability. The loss of a device has severe implications if agile workers choose to keep personal photos, data, or music on their devices and have not backed them up elsewhere.
- **Device lockdown**—allows IT support teams to decide what subsets of features are available on a device to an agile worker. For example, an agile worker may be allowed to use all installed applications, but may not be allowed to install any new ones, or may be allowed to use business applications, but may not be allowed to play games or use social media applications.
- **Antivirus software**—viruses and malicious software (malware) are also risks that need to be addressed. Most antivirus software vendors now offer solutions that include products for laptops, mobile devices, and tablets.

- **Total cloud environments**—operating in a full cloud environment negates the risks of losing data as files are hosted securely in data centers and are continuously backed up.

A more comprehensive and systematic mobile device security solution is provided by technologies such as enterprise mobile device management (MDM) and network access control (NAC). These technologies are like a remote control for employees' mobiles and can be used to manage smartphones, tablets, and notebooks, providing a single solution for multiple platforms if a device has been lost or stolen. For example, an MDM can:

- Lock the device remotely, or set/reset a pin code
- Locate the device remotely
- Wipe the device remotely
- Restore settings and preferences to a new device
- Restore Wi-Fi and VPN (virtual private network) settings to a new device
- Restore previously installed applications to a new device
- Restrict the capability of devices

The MDM approach can be regarded as device-centric security. In a data-centric security approach, apps and data can be partitioned, or apps can operate around the data. Personal and corporate data types can be kept separate. Corporate apps with sensitive data can be "sandboxed" off from other content in an encrypted container. If an agile worker downloads an app that contains malware, the malware cannot access the data inside the container.

Many IT teams are moving to a data-centric model for other aspects of enterprise infrastructure—data loss prevention, data centers, and database monitoring. Data-centric security provides agile workers with device choice and privacy while enabling IT with manageable policies and reliable control over sensitive data.

Organizations need to create a security culture and secure data among their employees. The importance of effective information management and the protection of privacy will be heightened by the introduction of the General Data Protection Regulation (GDPR), with significant penalties if it is not observed, as it will affect not only organizations in Europe but also those trading with Europe. The connection to the GDPR comes when Shadow IT introduces "unregistered data sources" to the organization, that is, data that is unknown to the data controller (the person legally responsible for the control, storage, and use of personal information held on IT systems). For example, an organization cannot honor a customer request to delete their personal data if this data is also stored on the employee's BYOD devices.

Good information governance is needed so that the vast quantity of information held is identified, managed, and secured. The information management processes should include policies and procedures, employee training, and information on compliance.

# CHAPTER 4

# Agile Working and the Modern Workplace

According to the Leesman Index, 85 percent of people surveyed say the design of their workplace is important to them.[1] Traditionally many offices were designed for only two activities: sitting at a desk or having meetings. However, as described in Chapter 1 activity-based working enables employees to undertake a range of distinct tasks in a more productive and enjoyable way.

In 2015 70 percent of all U.S. offices had an open design.[2] However, the standard commercial real estate lease can range between 10 and 15 years, but this can be seen as inflexible and problematic when technology can develop beyond recognition within five years. More agile organizations are likely to restructure three times during this lease period each time with different, and probably reduced, accommodation needs.

## Supporting Work Activities

A modern office building that supports agile working, and activity-based working in particular, typically has designated areas for agile workers to concentrate, collaborate, and create and the furniture and facilities to support these activities. Of course, not all work activities fall into these categories, and there is still the need to respond to phone inquiries and the day-to-day firefighting. These, and other administrative tasks, are a feature of many jobs. So a significant percentage of a building is likely to be occupied by shared desks, or "hot desks," where employees carry out routine but necessary activities.

---

[1] 2015 Q2. Leesman Review Issue 17.

[2] April 2015 "Office of the Future." HP.

However, these "3C activities" (collaborative, creative, and contemplative described below) are likely to contribute more added value to businesses than routine tasks and are described below.

### *Contemplative Activities*

Contemplative activities, or as some call it "considerative work," such as report writing, require reflection and concentration and are best done isolated from colleagues. Employees may choose to book a meeting room for their sole use but this may be a selfish option if meeting rooms are in high demand and the room may not have the right ambiance. There is a range of more suitable facilities that can be provided such as designated quiet areas, enclosed, or semi-enclosed spaces, sometimes, called modular huddle spaces, which can provide a refuge from noise and distraction. Where space is limited, the provision of acoustic phone booths, for making and receiving phone calls, can help to eliminate noise distractions for those that require concentration. Offices that are too quiet can also be unproductive and sound masking systems can be used to artificially raise background sound using speakers and are now in frequent use.

Some employees claim their home is a conducive environment for this activity and requests for occasional homeworking are justified on the need to escape the interruptions of colleagues. However contemplative homeworking requires a degree of self-discipline to eschew the distractions of the home such as housework, outstanding do-it-yourself (DIY) jobs, TV, and children (not necessarily in that order).

### *Collaboration*

Collaboration is by definition a group activity but more purposeful than creative activity. Facilities should encourage collaboration between members or different teams working together, including space for partner organizations, where this does not breach security or compliance considerations. There should also be more informal collaboration areas such as dining areas and communal lounges.

Of course, with today's technologies, as described in Chapter 3, not all collaboration activities require employees to be in the same location.

The sharing of documents and other materials can be achieved by the use of WebEx, or similar conferencing facilities, which can be particularly cost-effective where employees are located hundreds, or even thousands, of miles apart. There should, therefore, be teleconferencing and video-conferencing facilities to involve those agile workers that are not on site.

### *Creativity*

It is arguable whether creativity is a solo or group activity but, for many, creativity is associated with interacting with others through group activities such as brainstorming and problem solving. Organizations can provide creative areas within their premises, on the assumption that, if the environment that appeals to and inspires their employees, they can't help but be more creative and productive. But there is, of course, a cost in providing accommodation designated for this purpose.

Some people believe isolation is the best creative environment, taking themselves away from day-to-day routines. For example, finding a quiet spot in the garden, or going for a long walk, can spark creative thoughts. This desired isolation also requires electronic, as well as mental, isolation from today's always-connected world—resisting the temptation to check e-mails and social media every five minutes.

### *Shared Desks*

Shared desks, or "hotdesks," are often the most contentious feature of modern office accommodation. A shared desk area needs to be ergonomically well designed, and fit for purpose. Otherwise, employees will be reluctant to use the facility especially if the environment is inferior to the facilities they have previously enjoyed.

A shared desk area can merely be some touchdown points where employees can connect their portable device. Where equipment is provided, there should be no differentiation between the shared desks so an agile worker can be confident that the same technology is available regardless of which desk they book to use. At a practical level, there should be plenty of sockets to power agile workers' devices and charge those that they are not currently using.

Storage will be needed as employees will no longer be permitted to keep their belongings on their desk. Typically lockers should be provided for employees that are large enough for personal items such as coats and also cycle helmets and gym kit to promote healthy lifestyles. There will also need to be shared storage where teams can keep physical objects although most paper documents should be digitized.

### *Managing Shared Facilities*

All shared facilities including desks should be bookable through an electronic booking system so that agile workers do not waste time finding the facility they need when they visit the office. There should also be a built-in monitoring system with sanctions to discourage people from booking facilities that they decide not to use preventing others from making use of, which on some days may be a scarce facility. A common exception to the booking system is the touchdown area, which can be used more informally and is typically used for only short periods of time.

With space at a premium, buildings will evolve into hyper-flexible areas. The size of teams and their workspace requirements will fluctuate based on which tasks they are working. The workspace will need to reflect this flexibility. Rooms will serve different functions, and walls, floors, and ceilings will have embedded technology, which will allow them to change position depending on the activity.[3]

### *The Role of Furniture*

The design of the office should be dynamic, as business requirements change and the employees and activities to meet them will also change. Furniture is better to define work areas than using partitions, as it can be readily reconfigured as requirements change, for example, high-backed sofas can create a private meeting space without the need for a separate room. There are ergonomic chairs that will automatically adjust to make the user comfortable.

---

[3] Aderin-Pocock, M., A. Mamou-Mani, T. Burgess, L. Aitken, and E. Leclercq. 2016. "Future Living Report." *Samsung Smart Things.*

Staff well-being is an increasingly important consideration. Sitting at a desk for long periods of time is now recognized as unhealthy, and a benefit of an activity-based working approach is that it encourages employees to move around the office between different work settings. Furniture can be obtained to support healthy activities such as tables that support stand-up meetings and desks with adjustable height settings to reduce periods of sedentary work.

### *Heating, Lighting, and Ventilation Needs*

The general considerations for heating, lighting, and ventilation should be similar for all offices, but it is possible to provide agile workers with choices such as hot and cold zones, places that are well lit and those that have more subdued lighting. There are lighting control systems that allow zoning, presence, or absence, detection, and daylight linking. These settings can be assessed against the BREEAM standard, which is a method of evaluating, rating, and certifying the sustainability of buildings and includes a category for health and well-being. The settings should be tested with employees at an early stage, as employees will avoid areas where they do not feel comfortable, and facilities and furniture may be underutilized.

This increased focus on employee well-being has led to the development of the WELL Building Standard,[4] a certification that rates buildings on seven different criteria related to health and well-being, including indoor air quality, access to natural light, and how much a building's design encourages physical activity.

## Coworking

Despite the developments of technology to enable people to work independently regardless of their location, some firms, including those that sell collaborative software, are locating their employees at a single site to encourage physical interaction. Some companies are decreasing the floor area of workplaces on purpose with the goal of helping employees to have more "collisions" with their colleagues. The theory is that,

[4] https://wellcertified.com/

by packing people into local clusters, they will be more productive and more creative. One example is a pharmaceutical company that designed a new building so that its scientists will be closely located to each other to stimulate copying, collaboration, and competition—which they claim will promote productivity.

Some organizations are taking this approach a step further by not only locating their employees in centralized offices but also juxtaposing them next to conducive organizations to spark creative thoughts. In London's Kings Cross, Google has built offices adjacent to the Central Saint Martins art school. The proximity of these premises provides opportunities for Google's employees to interact with creative students attending the design college with the opportunity to be stimulated by external thought forces. This is but one aspect of the economies of "agglomeration" where firms cluster together for these and other economic benefits.

While some organizations will provide these areas within their own premises, others will identify appropriate independently managed coworking spaces to give more opportunities for developing ideas with employees from other organizations. This different approach to delivering creative environments is being adopted by organizations, such as Cisco, which is allowing and encouraging their employees to use coworking spaces. Coworking is a style of work, also known as "hoteling," where working people, not employed by the same organization, share a working environment, typically an office. In 2016, over half (54 percent) of North American companies had planned to implement hoteling.[5]

Agile-working employees and freelancers can rent spaces or desks on a daily, weekly, or monthly basis. Some areas may be provided with additional amenities, such as free parking, kitchen use, and gym access. Village Underground, an unconventional coworking space in London, uses train cars and shipping containers, to provide an urban setting for a creative community.

For employers, the use of coworking spaces reduces accommodation costs, while for employees travel to a nearby coworking space, often called a "hub," can reduce commuting and offers a solution to the

---

[5] April 2015, "Office of the Future." HP.

problem of isolation while working at home or escape the distractions of home. Advocates of coworking claim it generates synergy from ideas generated from a shared community of talented people working in the same space.

# CHAPTER 5

# Agile Working and Culture Change

*The one true constant in life is change.*

—Heraclitus of Ephesus c. 535 BC–475 BC

As the nature of work changes, organizations will need to accept that change is inevitable and put in place mechanisms that enable them to react quickly to change. The leadership team needs to ensure that employees recognize that change is important and necessary. Embracing technology is not sufficient. Organizations need to actively pursue technology to maintain competitive advantage and attract and maintain talent. This is by no means easy, especially for organizations that were established in a pre-digital age and therefore need to adjust or shift their organizational culture to keep up in today's digital world.

An organization's culture reflects beliefs and values that have become entrenched over the years and may have been linked to its initial success and prosperity. One of the most common resistances to change is the fear of change itself. Long-serving employees are likely to resist change. If some employees have spent a significant proportion of their working life traveling to the same office at the same time, then suddenly finding themselves with a choice of working locations can be unsettling for them. People can fear change even when it is likely to be positive. Resisting change may also be rational if an employee feels that their status, even identity, is lost when they lose an assigned desk. Newly formed organizations, with management and employees unencumbered by traditions, can much more readily adopt an agile working and digital workspace model. It is not as if the world of work is perfect. A recent SHRM (Society for

Human Resource Management) survey[1] found that only 37 percent of U.S. employees were "very satisfied" with their jobs. So there is considerable potential to increase employees' job satisfaction through the introduction of agile working.

## Overcoming Resistance to New Ways of Working

Traditional organizations can often have many layers of management to control processes. These organizations may also show a tendency to overmanage how employees collaborate and network. Managers will need to recognize that the value of work is about measuring outputs and outcomes rather than time spent on a task. For agile working to be successful, employees need to be trusted by their managers, and also by their colleagues, and management should, within reasonable boundaries, encourage spontaneity and innovation, which, in turn, can lead to increases in productivity. When employees are free to experiment, and failures are considered learning opportunities, new ways of working will be discovered.

For organizations where managing by results is not the norm then both managers and employees will need to be educated to understand the new management culture. Trust is key to agile working. Managers will need to be confident that in return for giving them greater autonomy their employees will be more responsive in meeting their work commitments. Through a change in culture employees who are working in a more autonomous way will feel valued and supported.

Building a thriving agile working culture supported by a digital workspace works best when all employees share an understanding of the benefits to themselves as well as to the organization. And this buy-in has to be from all levels of the organization. Agile working is a journey; there is no defined endpoint and a culture of constant change will need to be established if the organization is to continue moving forward. Agile workers, as well as management, should continually challenge existing processes and approaches to see how they can be improved. The leadership team of the

[1] "Employee Job Satisfaction and Engagement. 2016." The Society For Human Resource Management.

organization will need to demonstrate the need for change and maintain the momentum.

A key factor to successfully embedding agile working into an organization is removing a culture of presenteeism. Presenteeism is the result of a lack of trust, which is a great inhibitor to a results-based agile working culture. Many employees believe they have to be sitting at a desk so they can be seen to be working, even that they may be overlooked for promotion if they are not visible. Managers, and sometimes colleagues of agile workers, may be fearful or need reassurance that employees working at home are working as intensely as they would be in the office—or even working at all! However a survey by Jobsite[2] found that 85 percent of candidates do not believe agile working will damage their career prospects, with 35 percent saying that they would expect to progress faster in these environments.

Successful agile working cannot be dictated by policy, but with education and involvement employees will voluntarily commit to agile working through a program of workforce communication and engagement. When employees understand and appreciate the reasons behind the new way of working, explained in a way relevant to them, with the benefits it offers employees, they are far more likely to support it.

The successful adoption of agile working requires a change in workplace behaviors that is delivered through a cogent explanation of the agile working solution and suitable learning based on individuals' needs. In my experience running facilitated workshops for managers and employees to introduce the concept and examine the practicalities is an excellent way of overcoming resistance.

*Some changes required for agile working are low level and practical. For example, where space is shared by team members, the presumption that the "owned" workspace remains as set up by a user is no longer valid. It needs to be recognized that people using the same group of desks will inevitably set up the workspace to suit their needs, readjusting monitor alignment, and the height of the chair. The exception will be those employees*

[2] "Recruiting for the Agile Workforce. November 2017." Jobsite survey.

*with disabilities or other recognized requirements as having special needs. Where necessary, specified furniture and equipment can be dedicated to these employees.*

## Overcoming Resistance to the Digital Workspace

Digital workspace requires employees adopting ways of working that are more collaborative, open, and based on principles of trust and sharing. While there is no shortage of digital tools to support the digital workspace the take-up has been far from rapid. Only a small number of employees can currently be called digital natives and, while these tools are relatively easy to use, much of the workforce remains committed to its nondigital ways of working.

In a Gartner Research 2016 survey of 3,120 enterprise workers, 52 percent said they use very little digital technology, 41 percent said their digital skills have no impact on business success, and 36 percent had never been asked their opinion on digital technology use. The research also showed many managers actively discouraging workers from using technology. Forty-four percent of respondents said they were discouraged from using technology to improve business outcomes and a further 42 percent said their managers showed no interest in using technology to improve outcomes.

Here are some examples of the persistence of nondigital ways of working; much has to do with custom and practice.

### *Paper-Based Working*

Even with the extensive deployment of tablets and lightweight laptops, many will still attend meetings with paper notepad to take notes. So why does this matter? It boils down to personal and corporate productivity. If notes are written on paper, they need to be transcribed into electronic documents before they are accessible to other people. In the past, they may have been photocopied for distribution, but at least this has become an environmental no-no. While many people may initially find the use of screen-based information an unwelcome change from using printed documents, there are applications, such as OneNote, which replicate and enhance the features of paper-based note-taking.

Although an increasing number of people are working away from their office base, many still prefer to take paper documents with them. However not only is carrying heavy paper documents, compared to a lightweight laptop or tablet, uncomfortable, their movement also introduces security risks. We still regularly hear of incidents where important documents have been left on trains or have been snapped by the press.

Many people still prefer to print out paper copies to review documents, claiming reading paper is more comfortable on their eyes—and the now faltering sales of e-readers and tablets perhaps supports this argument. If the documentation is shredded after it has been reviewed, that is one thing, but there is often a strong human desire to store documents. Apart from generating unnecessary printing costs, there is the question of storage. Filing cabinets take up floor space and space costs money, especially if it is occupying offices in a prime location.

### *Encouraging Digital Working*

For an organization to achieve digitalization, it is as much to do with changing the culture than it is about employees learning to use new digital tools. Culture change will come from a combination of leadership, employees' self-interest, and practical measures.

While managers need to set the example by showing how their teams can work digitally, they also need to promote the benefits of the digital workspace. There are practical carrot and stick approaches such as the tried and tested method of reducing the number of printers, so employees have the inconvenience of finding an available printer to retrieve printouts while ensuring employees have access to a sufficiently large screen, so they don't have to squint to read documents.

People need confidence and competence to work digitally and the opportunity to develop their digital skills. The UK Government Skills Strategy has recently been launched with the aim of "Giving everyone access to the digital skills they need." Most people are not starting from ground zero. Many can draw on their experience of online shopping and banking and use Twitter and Skype for their personal and family activities.

Employees regularly have digital experiences in their personal and social activities and often enjoy the ease of use, personalization, and time-saving benefits. These benefits need to be matched in the digital workspace provided by the organization that employs them.

### *Replacing Physical Meetings with Virtual Meetings*

Conferencing technologies can enhance productivity by allowing people to participate from any location through an Internet connection and only involve them when they are required to participate resulting in shorter more focused meetings. They can also contribute to the bottom line through business travel savings and a reduced requirement for meeting rooms. Conferencing technologies have a mixed record of success depending on the type of meeting for which they are employed.

From work that the author has undertaken with clients, the following types of meetings are regarded as suitable to be held as virtual meetings, although there is a view that a proportion, say one in four sessions, should be kept as face-to-face meetings to maintain personal contact.

- 1:1 meetings, for example, objective setting
- Budget meetings
- Client-contractor meetings
- Departmental meetings
- Project meetings
- Internal meetings
- Meetings with partner organizations

There are a number of meeting types that are regarded as not suitable to be held as virtual meetings:

- "Town Hall meetings" or "Away Days" where personal and social contacts are essential features of these events.
- Conferences—while webinars are increasingly used and are an efficient use of employees' time there are advantages to participants in attending occasional physical conferences as they provide opportunities for networking.

- Meetings that involve personal issues, for example, appraisals, disciplinary meetings. In these meetings, physical presence is necessary to conduct the meetings appropriately and sensitively.
- Where a meeting is expected to engender hostility or negative feedback it is likely to be better managed as a physical meeting.
- Coaching and mentoring—on balance the view prevails that it is better to conduct these activities in person, although some organizations have provided them through collaborative technologies.

Below the five principal meeting types are identified and described, and the most suitable conferencing technologies recommended.

1. **Status Update Meetings**
   Status update meetings are concerned with establishing progress on a project or new initiative and ensuring that decisions are communicated to the team or group. The sessions are usually sharply focused and consequently brief. Conferencing technologies are regularly used for the status update meetings, which are typically held weekly. The disruption and travel costs of holding physical status update meetings are rarely justified. An audioconference is usually sufficient as the participants are likely to meet regularly.
2. **Decision-making Meetings**
   While minor decisions may be taken in a status update meeting, it is often necessary to call a specific meeting to agree more significant decisions. Conferencing technology scores here; meetings can be called at reasonably short notice, as people will not need to travel to attend the meeting. Screensharing is often required so that the participants have access to the latest documentation describing the situation.
3. **Information-sharing Meetings**
   These meetings can range from informal briefings to a small group of people to more formal presentations to a large number of participants. For informal gatherings, conferencing technology is suitable

and again has the advantage of being able to set up the meeting at short notice.

For more formal meetings a webinar will usually be more appropriate where leaders of the meeting can share slides, video, and other materials with their audience. Rather than being passive listeners, participants can use the facilities of the webinar tool to provide views and comments during the webinar. The presenter can also respond to the feedback during the presentation making the meeting a more engaging experience.

4. **Problem-solving and Collaborative Meetings**

These meetings are less focused than decision-making meetings. The problem or opportunity may not be apparent and often there is the need to think "outside of the box." These types of meetings are still more commonly held as a physical meeting as this is believed to encourage commitment and develop a creative atmosphere. Videoconferencing is likely to be the most appropriate technology, as it should ensure partitipation and body language, and other indicators, can be taken into account. Sufficient time will need to be made available for the issues and options to be identified and thoroughly discussed.

Video and other information can be shared through the conferencing system to set the scene and help participants to understand the issues. Feedback mechanism tools, where responses can be anomymized for sensitive issues, will be a more efficient of people's time than the traditional "going around the table" to elicit people's views. Many conferencing systems have recording facilities that can be used to make sure all points discussed are captured.

5. **Consultations**

Traditionally seeking the views of people you have not met before has been done through face-to-face meetings, as people feel more comfortable introducing themselves in person and the comforting tactile feel of a real handshake. However, this can be an expensive way of gathering information and views. In reality, an hour's meeting can take half a day when traveling to and from the consultee's place of work is taken into account. Sometimes a physical meeting is just not possible; a colleague of mine has been conducting an assignment from the UK with a client based in Australia. Apart from having to work late at night because of the time difference, this has worked well.

In summary,

- **Audioconferencing** was seen as suitable for meetings that involve short updates or quick decisions.
- **Videoconferencing** was felt to be more suited for more serious discussions as participants could see body language and facial expressions. It was also more effective in involving remote participants and is often thought to fit better for organizations that have a people-focused culture.
- **Screensharing** is often needed for virtual meetings, as many meetings require documents to be viewed and amended collaboratively.

Creating the right collaboration culture from the top is important. Two-thirds of respondents of the Harvard survey agreed that C-level executives should lead the corporate culture of collaboration but only half said that happened in reality.[3] If leadership is not engaged in the use of a new digital workplace, it will be difficult to encourage the rest of the workforce. It is important to engage and enthuse potential users of the digital workplace. Their needs can be established through discovery processes and user testing. Their feedback will be particularly valuable.

## MultiGenerational Workforce

The workforce of today and tomorrow will comprise a number of generations each with different attitudes to work and experience of technology as Table 5.1 shows.

Later generations have more experience of technology and are more likely to embrace the digital workspace. By 2020, Millennials will comprise at least half of the global workforce, and Generation Z will make up

[3] "Analytic Services Survey. August 2016." *Harvard Business Review.*

H13

*Table 5.1 The multigenerational workforce*

| Generation | Characteristics |
|---|---|
| **Traditionalist** | |
| Born | Before 1946 |
| Attitude to life | Personal responsibility very important |
| Attitude to work | Position and authority important |
| Familiarity with technology | Only the telephone in use while growing up |
| **Baby boomers** | |
| Born | Between 1946 and 1964 |
| Attitude to life | Pursue success and prosperity |
| Attitude to work | "Live to work" |
| Familiarity with technology | Prefer face-to-face communication and interaction |
| **Generation X** | |
| Born | Between 1965 and 1980 |
| Attitude to life | Resourceful and adaptable, family life important |
| Attitude to work | "Works to live," seek responsibility and creativity |
| Familiarity with technology | Tech-savvy and open to change |
| **Generation Y** | **Aka "Millennials"** |
| Born | Between 1980 and 2000 |
| Attitude to life | Individualistic |
| Attitude to work | Participative, goal-oriented, and enjoy multitasking |
| Familiarity with technology | Grew up with computers and the Internet |
| **Generation Z** | |
| Born | After 2000 |
| Attitude to life | Expectation of instantaneous gratification |
| Attitude to work | Easy acceptance of new ideas |
| Familiarity with technology | Grew up with a mobile device and want their devices to be "always on" and natural skills in technology |

35 percent of the workforce.[4] There will, of course, be a shift over time to the later generations as younger employees are recruited. However, as many employees postpone retirement, there will be as many as five generations in the workforce.

Of course, categorizing employees by their generation is over simplistic as there are undoubtedly many other attributes to consider including

[4] "Office of the Future. April 2015." HP.

their personality types as discussed in Chapter 11. However, organizations that understand how to draw successfully on each generation's strengths will be better able to keep employees motivated and productive.

## Work–Life Integration and Workwrapping

An example of a win-win situation for organizations and their employees in new ways of working is workwrapping. First, a short history of work–life balance. For employees in traditional nine-to-five office working and shift workers, there was a clear separation between time spent working and not working. With the advent of flexible working time boundaries for work became movable. The location of work also became flexible. What had been an apparent division between time spent "at work" and time away from work now needed defining. The term work–life balance was coined, setting boundaries between "worktime," that is, activities undertaken for your employer and "non-worktime" for personal and social activities. Work–life balance has been around since the year 2000 and is now a commonly understood concept (try the work–life balance quiz at the end of this chapter).

For employees work–life balance was perceived as an employment benefit and provided an assurance that work requirements would not encroach on their personal time. However, work–life balance is now out of kilter. People's behavior has changed with the advent of new technologies. Personal devices, such as tablets and smartphones, have become an intrinsic part of our personal lives. For many, it is natural to take these devices into the work environment. Regardless of whether or not their employer has a "bring your own device policy" they are now commonly used for work activities as well as for personal use. As a consequence, we have ready access to business, as well as personal, information and systems. A research[5] by the Chartered Institute of Personnel and Development found that 40 percent of people check work e-mails at least five times a day outside of working hours and almost a third say remote access to work means they can never fully switch off, while Regus found that

[5] "Employee Views on Working Life. Spring 2017." cipd.co.uk/employeeoutlook

39 percent of employees will be working up to three hours each day while on holiday.[6] These are the phenomena of today's working practices.

Work–life integration is a new and much less understood, and sometimes resisted, term. Work–life integration is a concept linked to agile working. Rather than being imposed by employers, it is being adopted by employees and is partly the consequence of technological developments. As lighter weight "BYOD" personal devices, such as tablets and powerful smartphones, are easy to carry, they are nearly always to hand and have become an essential part of our modern lives. As a consequence, we have ready access to business, as well as personal, information and systems.

Apart from mixing personal and business information on the same device many people are now mixing their business and personal time. It is entirely feasible to undertake personal/social activities in "worktime" and working activities in "non-worktime" and the work–life balance boundary has become porous. Within the space of a few minutes, we can check our business and personal e-mails, check the weather forecast, book business travel, or book a table at a restaurant. In this new way of working, sometimes also called a connected lifestyle, work–life balance is replaced by work–life integration. However, the concept of work–life integration has encountered strong resistance from some employees who regard it as an intrusion of work responsibilities into their personal life. Some claim they feel, like their devices that they are "always on," receiving e-mails and other communications, in the evening and at weekends with an obligation to respond to them immediately. In essence, they feel work–life integration tilts the balance in favor of work. For example, if their mobile device continues to "ping" the arrival of new e-mails all evenings and all weekends employees can feel they are "always on" and this can lead to stress.

However, this ready access to information can be turned to the advantage of agile workers if they embrace "workwrapping" and restore a new dynamic type of work–life balance that offers greater choices in the way we work. Workwrapping redresses the work–life balance but in a more subtle and dynamic way. It exploits the opportunities provided by agile

[6] The demographics of Flexible Working Regus—June 2015.

working practices that are being increasingly adopted by employing organizations. With agile working, performance is explicitly based on objective measures of output provided they fulfill the business requirements; agile workers can choose how, as well as when and where, they carry out their work activities. This increased autonomy in the way employees can work means that, in many cases, employees can prioritize their time.

What if you prioritized your personal activities and wrapped work activities around high-priority social and personal activities? As a simple example, if you have a report to write by the end of the week, and the sun is shining, you could decide to have an impromptu family picnic. Alternatively, if you find you are spending a lot of time queuing in a theme park waiting to get on the rides, you could decide to clear some outstanding e-mails while you are waiting. It could be argued that planning to divide time between work and nonwork activities is quite a common practice already, but workwrapping takes this a step further by dynamically allocating all available time between work and nonwork activities. For example, if the sun is shining why not enjoy it and write that report after the sun disappears?

In reality, many employed senior professionals and managers already enjoy considerable discretion in when and where they work and are measured on outcomes and the quality of their work. Outside of the employed world, consultants and other self-employed professionals have adopted this concept, if not the name workwrapping. They often choose to work evenings and weekends and substitute some weekday time for social activities. They have also recognized the benefits of addressing issues as and when they occur, even when they had not planned to be working, as "nipping them in the bud" can prevent problems escalating.

But what of those jobs that have a time presence requirement, such as classroom teachers? In reality, a number of professions will have output-based elements where there is a choice of when these tasks can be done, for example, in the case of teaching, lesson preparation and marking of students' work. More generally many professions have output-based activities such as report writing.

The physical presence of operational roles is also being rethought. For example, take the role of a receptionist. They do not need to sit at a reception desk. Many small businesses, which cannot afford a full-time receptionist, often provide a call button system, sometimes supported by CCTV, to alert employees so they can greet visitors via an intercom. This enables reception staff to be more productive by being able to undertake additional "back office" activities. Looking to the future within the next 10 years, intelligent software agents will reduce the time presence required for monitoring and control while robots will increasingly be used for activities that currently require physical presence. The opportunities for work wrapping can only increase.

Workwrapping is a challenge for employers and employees. For employees, the trade-off for more flexibility in working time is accepting greater responsibility in meeting work commitments. For employers, the trade-off for employees becoming more responsible and responsive is adopting a relaxed attitude to their employees' working practices, particularly to when employees choose to work. With the fuzzy boundaries of work–life integration, this new way of working could cut across established HR practices such as defined working hours and annual leave entitlement. However, workwrapping can be a win-win situation: employees can prioritize their time for social and family priorities and with the focus on clearly defined outputs employees can become more productive.

## Work–Life Balance Questionnaire

1. **How would you describe your personal work ethos?**
   (a) I live and breathe work
   (b) I tend to start early/leave late
   (c) I do as much as I can in the time that I have
   (d) I complete the necessary evil to avoid being sacked
2. **Do you ever find yourself working during your time off (holidays/weekends)?**
   (a) Always
   (b) Only when necessary
   (c) Not really—holidays and weekends are my own
   (d) Never—I don't get paid enough
3. **How would you describe the atmosphere at work?**
   (a) Stressful and pressurized

(b) Focused on results
(c) Industrious but not overbearing
(d) Easygoing and relaxed

4. **How much stress is there within your working environment?**
(a) Too much
(b) Lots—particularly when deadlines are looming
(c) Sometimes stress is apparent but not often
(d) None

5. **Does your work affect your social life/time outside of work?**
(a) Always
(b) Now and then
(c) I try not to mix work with my own time
(d) No—work enhances my social life

6. **How would you rate your ability to balance your working and social commitments**
(a) Badly
(b) Not as good as it should be
(c) Average
(d) Excellent

7. **Have you ever considered a "break" from your career?**
(a) Never had time
(b) Have considered it—maybe when the time is right
(c) Yes—a break is part of my plan
(d) Yes—I intend to break and not come back

8. **Can you discuss your work/life balance with your manager?**
(a) No—we tend to discuss work issues at all times
(b) Not sure—never really discussed work/life balance before
(c) Yes—my manager actively encourages my work/life balance
(d) I tend to avoid my manager as much as possible

### *RESPONSES*

*(Mostly "A"s)* **Chill out!—before stress takes its toll!**
Perhaps you should consider taking a step back from your working environment and assess whether you are achieving any work/life balance. Your answers indicate you are used to high levels of stress that in

turn could lead to the following: exhaustion, poor working results, lack of focus, family and personal difficulties, and mental illness. Although working hard may be deemed necessary in your current environment, you should perhaps ask yourself whether this is all you want from life.

*(Mostly "B"s)* **Pace yourself!—your work–life balance is out of kilter!** You work hard, and you probably realize you should have more leisure time. You may have more work to complete than time to finish it, and as a result you work more hours just to get the job done. However, with new initiatives being introduced to encourage effective work/life balance, the hours you spend at work may soon change for the better.

*(Mostly "C"s)* **Congratulations!—you're a well-balanced individual!** Who wouldn't be jealous? You have worked out the work/life balance issues that have left personnel practitioners pulling their hair out for years. You seem to have found a balance between your working commitments and personal life. You demonstrate an awareness of the benefits of maintaining your work and personal life, so well done.

Can you share your secret?

*(Mostly "D"s)* **You're laid back!—but are you pulling your weight?** It would appear to be the case that you have a relaxed working situation. However, what you may need to remember is that in every working environment a certain level of stress is expected. Indeed, some people feel the need for an element of stress to achieve the best result and being overly comfortable at work is not always regarded as healthy.

# PART III

# Embarking on the Agile Working Journey

An assessment of an organization's agile working readiness is a crucial step in preparing for the successful implementation of this new way of working, identifying not only barriers but also opportunities.

Building a strong business case is the best way to articulate why any transformation is necessary. In reality, many projects are kicked off without a business case but a business case, at an appropriate level of detail, will provide an essential reference point to remind everyone of the objectives and the benefits of the agile working initiative when the going gets tough.

To obtain the benefits of this new way of working an organization will need to develop an agile working strategy to address the people, processes, and technology opportunities and issues. All these elements need to be aligned with the shared vision and agreed strategy.

While agile working should be considered as a journey where current ways of working are continuously challenged, and further opportunities for improvements are sought, many agile working initiatives start as a project or program. The agile working program needs to be set up in the right way with good governance and a strong program team drawn from a number of disciplines. An effective Communications and Engagement Plan is a critical success factor.

Agile working draws on a range of disciplines, so when it comes to implementing the agile working program it will be more manageable to break the program down into a number of workstreams, which are related to the disciplines of HR, IT, estates and facilities management, and so on.

# CHAPTER 6

# Assessing Agile Working Readiness

Before embarking on an agile working journey, it is helpful to gather information to form an understanding of the current working activities and employee attitudes to ways of working within the organization. The opportunity should also be taken to assess the suitability of the physical facilities and current technology to support new ways of working. Information can be gathered in a number of ways.

## Consultations

It is necessary to distinguish between enabling departments and operational departments.

**Enabling departments** are the key departments, such as HR, IT, and real estate and facilities management that will enable and support the agile working initiative.

**Operational departments** will be the primary beneficiaries of agile working, but in the consultation process the opportunity should be given to provide them with a clear understanding of the concepts and benefits of agile working. The consultations should address the practicalities for those departments adopting agile working.

Through these consultations, it should be possible to identify the barriers and issues associated with agile working with factors that would support the introduction of agile working. These discussions also help to identify those individuals and teams with a vested interest in the initiative and whose actions could directly impact the successfulness of the outcome. Some of the most critical stakeholders in an agile working initiative are the organization's employees. Through a discovery process, an understanding and clear insight into employee engagement and current working practices can be determined.

## Tools to Assess Readiness

There are a number of tools and approaches that can be used to acquire information and hard data about the organization's readiness for agile working.

There are three principal methods of consultation:

- **Interviews**—this is the most time-consuming approach so this is suited to a small number of people such as senior managers and key players.
- **Workshops/focus groups**—provide opportunities to debate issues with current ways of working and concerns about new ways of working.
- **Employee surveys**—offer an inclusive form of consultation as they provide the opportunity for all employees to state their views on current and proposed ways of working. Apart from capturing employees' current ways of working it is useful to capture:
    - Employees' existing knowledge of agile working and other new ways of working
    - Any benefits they have identified with agile working
    - Concerns they have about agile working
    - How suitable they believe their role is to agile working
    - The current levels of trust and autonomy they are given by their manager
    - Their reliance on colleagues to undertake their work tasks
    - Their views of current technology provision
    - Their skills and knowledge of technologies that will be used in the digital workspace

A summary of the findings of the survey should be fed back to employees so they can see their views have been noted and how their views compare to those of their colleagues.

### *Space Utilization Study*

A space utilization study is undertaken to provide evidence of how and when premises are being used by the occupants across the working week. Apart from establishing how well existing facilities are used, a study may also provide information about current workstyles and can prepare for the introduction of changes to working practices.

> *As much as two-thirds of all workspaces are unoccupied during working hours because of holidays, illness, employees attending training courses, meetings, and offsite visits.*

A space utilization study can provide hard data to answer the following questions:

- How is the space (desks, meeting rooms, breakout spaces, and other communal areas) being used?
- Who is using the space?—broken down by department, team, and job role.
- How does use vary between days of the week times during the day?
- Which areas are more popular than others?
- What areas are underused?

There are many ways of conducting space utilization studies, but they have been classified into three ways by the World Customs Organization (WCO)[1]:

- Observation studies—where a team records the use of meeting spaces of observers.
- Automated data collection—using monitoring devices such as those on turnstiles, movement sensors using the computers' IP addresses.

---

[1] Nigel Oseland (Editor), Nicola Gillen, Germain Verbeemen, Meirion Anderson, Paul Allsopp, and Bridget Hardy. April 2013. "The WCO Guide to: Utilisation and Occupancy Studies." Occasional Paper OP3, v1.4.

- People tracking—where the activities of employees are monitored by observation or recorded by the employees themselves.

A more detailed analysis of building occupancy, as illustrated in Figure 6.1, can show:

- The computer on the desk is actively being used for **work**, that is, the employee has logged on and is actively using their computer.
- The computer on the desk is not actively being used for work and is **locked**, for example, the employee is present but away from their desk, for example, attending a meeting.
- The computer on the desk is **idle**, that is, the employee has not logged on and is likely not to be at the desk.

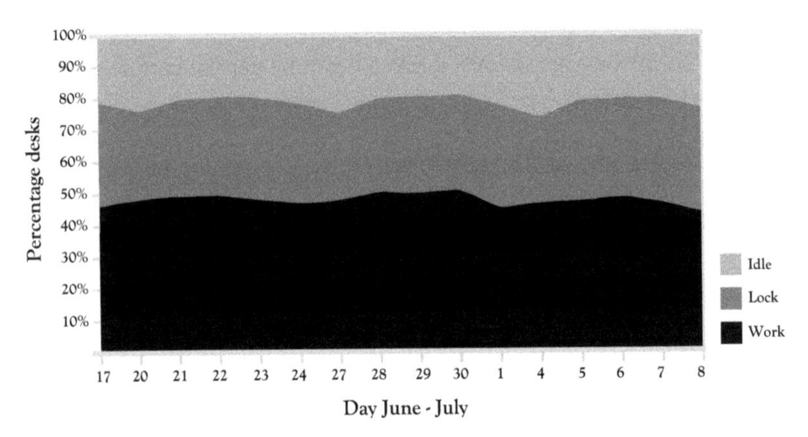


*Figure 6.1 Building occupancy example*

## Technology Review

The technology requirements of agile working readiness are about much more than determining the appropriate devices agile workers should use to fit their workstyle. For employees to be confident in being able to work wherever they are; the infrastructure, data and voice, will need to be reliable, accessible, and provide secure connections at suitable speeds. A review of current and planned IT provision should be carried out to assess how suited IT provision is able to support the agile working initiative. This review should cover:

- **Connectivity for data and voice**—to establish the criteria for speed, performance, reliability, and resilience for communications over the network. Agile working relies on a robust IT infrastructure including applications and storage in the cloud so that employees have to be able to connect quickly from a range of locations. The availability and resilience of Wi-Fi are often critical factors.
- **IT service provision and support arrangements**—to establish if additional provision is needed to support employees working in an agile working environment.
- **Security of data and systems**—to ensure how the additional risks from agile working of data loss and unauthorized access to data can be addressed.
- **Device deployment and management**—to assess how and on what basis devices are deployed and how the use of employees' own devices and shadow IT is managed.
- **Line-of-business application systems**—to assess whether critical systems can be readily accessed remotely and that their performance is not significantly impacted when used remotely.
- **Conferencing, collaboration, and communication tools**—what tools are provided?
- **Document and information management**—to assess how information is managed so it can be readily accessed by employees with appropriate authority and securely stored. Is "follow me" printing available so agile workers by swiping a card can print from any of the organization's printers?
- **IT skills of agile workers**—what training is provided to equip employees with the skills and knowledge to use systems with minimal support?

## Review of Policies

Agile working requires different working practices and is likely to have an impact on many existing policies for the organization and so a good starting point is to identify and review all the policies that might impact on the new ways of working. The policies that may need revision are identified in Chapter 10.

## Summarizing the Findings

The findings from the readiness review should be summarized in a current position report. An analysis broken down by work practices, workspace, technology, and culture can be summarized under the headings of:

- Supporting factors for new ways of working
- Issues and concerns

Misconceived concerns should be identified and addressed as soon as possible while real concerns and issues should be captured for later consideration. True "blockers" to the implementation of agile working will need to be thought through to see how they can be overcome with new, often more imaginative, approaches.

In working with a range of clients, we have identified a number of factors that are key indicators of agile working readiness of your organization.

- Identifying flexible workspaces—not all the workspaces need to be owned by the organization, but they could be commercially provided work hubs, or the use, by arrangement, of suitably equipped premises of partner organizations
- Reliable infrastructure
- Employees' confidence and competence in their use of digital technologies
- A "Can do" culture measuring outputs and outcomes rather than time spent on a task

- A culture of trust between managers and employees and between employees

When these readiness factors are in place, the organization will have a good chance of implementing agile working successfully.

# CHAPTER 7

# Making the Business Case for Agile Working

In constructing the business case, it is best to take an organization-wide view to identify areas where agile working could best increase effectiveness and meet the strategic aims of the organization. This view should be tempered with a realistic assessment of business readiness for new ways of working as described in the preceding chapter.

Some organizations will view a business case purely in financial terms to establish there is a return on their investment, for example, they would have surplus property that they can dispose of by sale, or renting out, as a consequence of adopting agile working. Others will take a Return on Objectives approach to demonstrate that the goals they set can be achieved. These goals may be a range of non-cashable benefits such as:

- Promote and support employee well-being.
- Provide improved customer service.
- Optimize productivity and performance through a team-based approach.
- Focus on people, not property, taking full advantage of the innovative estates transformation.
- Promote the organization as a recognizable modern, forward-thinking employer.
- Create a working environment that attracts and retains a motivated workforce.
- "Spaceless growth" so the organization can increase its number of employees without incurring a proportionate increase in property costs.
- Promote the organization's corporate social responsibility taking account of the social, economic, and environmental impact on the organization.

*The Agile Future Forum and McKinsey & Company researched[1] the financial benefits of adopting agile working and their studies demonstrated benefits equivalent to 3–13 percent of workforce costs. Furthermore, they believe that more extensive or innovative agile working practices could generate further value of 3–7 percent of workforce cost.*

## The Drivers for Agile Working

While there are many benefits of adopting agile working, it is essential to identify and understand the drivers that will commit an organization to embrace the change. Without clear drivers, with an accompanying vision and goal, the organization is unlikely to maintain the momentum needed to overcome the challenges of implementing agile working.

Typical drivers of an agile working program are cited in Figure 7.1.

Each will have business benefits associated with them, but only three or four of these will be the drivers for an organization's adoption of agile working.

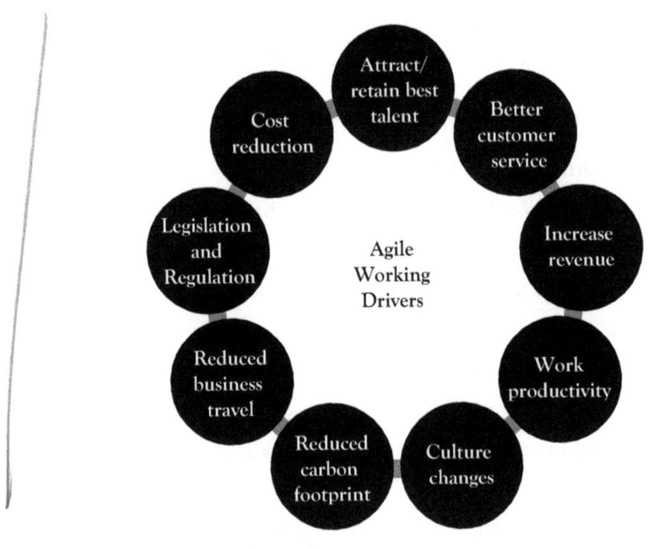


***Figure 7.1 Agile working drivers***

[1] The Agile Future Forum. June 2013. "Understanding the Economic Benefits of Workforce Agility."

## The Benefits of Agile Working to the Organization

> *Care should be taken not to claim business benefits that have already been allocated to another program. An agile working program is likely to cut across other initiatives with dependencies between them. The agile working program should not be seen as in competition with other projects as it can often bring additional benefits to them by promoting new ways of working.*

The adoption of agile working can provide many tangible benefits for organizations as listed here.

### *Performance Improvement and Productivity*

Agile working is correlated with performance improvement through more efficient and effective ways of working.

### *Improvements in Workforce Productivity*

Agile working is associated with productivity improvement through more efficient and effective ways of working. For example, by providing a range of more appropriate workspaces for tasks employees will be able to increase the quantity and/or quality of their outputs. There are a number of measures in which performance improvement can be expressed as described in Chapter 1.

There is likely to be increased productivity from self-organizing, motivated employees who feel empowered to choose how, where, and when they work. Team-based productivity should increase, through greater interaction, collaboration, and knowledge sharing. With employees no longer tied to their desks, there's likely to be more communication and collaboration across teams and business functions those who need to concentrate will experience less distraction. There should be consequent productivity gains from more innovatory processes and higher quality output.

Salaries and benefits account for around 90 percent of the operating costs of a typical large business, so modest increases in productivity can have a significant impact on the bottom line.

## Reduced Business Travel

Investments in technology including videoconferencing will enable a large number of physical meetings to be replaced by virtual meetings, with a consequential reduction in the cost of attending physical meetings. There may also be further travel savings where videoconferencing is used in training course so that "trainees" do not need to travel to a classroom.

Employees who need to travel to attend physical meetings and appointments to clients and customers can plan their journeys efficiently to manage their visits. Some employees may be able to start from and, return to, their home rather than beginning and completing their working day at an office base. Furthermore, the provision of touchdown and other agile working facilities will enable agile workers to continue working at the location of the meeting rather than having to return to base.

The value of the time saved is the reduction in the time spent traveling to meetings times the average cost per hour of employees' time spent traveling (e.g., for car travel this would be the average distance traveled at a typical average speed). However, the overall total mileage may increase if the average number of daily contacts is increased as a consequence of these employees adopting agile working. In this case, an estimate of the travel mileage per client contact would be a better measure of the saving rather than total distance traveled.

With reduced travel, there is also a cash saving in the reduced costs of the employees' travel expenses, car mileage and car parking, public transport costs, and in some cases hotel accommodation.

Agile workers traveling by public transport can save time. They can undertake some work activities, for example, sending and reading e-mails, editing documents while they are on the move. However, from their duty of care responsibilities, employers should not expect employees to make or receive phone calls while driving. The use of phones by employees traveling on public transport should be discouraged as it may raise security issues as well as annoying fellow travelers.

## Reduced Absenteeism

Evidence from many case studies has shown that organizations that have adopted agile working and flexible working have seen reductions in ad-hoc sickness absence (i.e., occasional sickness leave for a day or weeks). Agile working reduces the need for employees to take leave for minor home-based issues such as waiting in for an engineer to call at their house or staying at home with a child with a minor illness.

Also, agile working promotes a less sedentary workstyle resulting in a healthier workforce with less chance of cancers, heart disease, and diabetes and, arguably, less longer-term absence through illness.

In addition, to maintain productivity, reductions in absenteeism will reduce the pressure on colleagues who would have to cover their colleagues' absence.

*A practical example—internal meetings. We can all agree there are too many meetings but in reality many are necessary where decisions are made on a consensus basis, such as in local government, so some meetings are a necessity. Physical meetings are inefficient in a number of ways. As offices shrink and people work in different locations finding a time when everyone can be in the same location can often incur delays before a meeting can be held. Attending meetings often requires travel, adding time and incurring costs. Physical meetings can often be longer than necessary—people arrive late or engage in conversations that are social or off the subject of the meeting. Not everyone attending is involved in every agenda item. If you use your laptop during a physical meeting, for example, to respond to e-mails or write a report, this is at best distracting to the other attendees and is often regarded as bad manners.*

*The digital equivalent of a physical meeting is a conference call. It involves no travel, not even walking down the corridor. As there are no travel arrangements to be made, conference calls can be held at quite short notice as it just depends on the availability of the participants. Participants can continue to work on e-mails and reports when they are not involved in the agenda item without disturbing anyone. In my experience, virtual meetings keep to the point and are invariably shorter than their physical equivalent.*

### Service Improvement

Agile working provides a number of opportunities for service improvement through the flexibility when services can be provided.

- Customers do not need to wait until employees are back in the office to answer their question, instead employees can log into their device and respond to it where they are.
- Services can be provided over extended business hours, as some employees will offer to work before or after the standard working day.
- It should be possible to match fluctuating demand for services as agile workers should be willing to work when demand for their skills is high instead of constraining their working hours to a rigid work pattern.
- For services that are delivered in the field agile workers can spend more time with their clients, as they need to spend less time traveling to and from their base office.

### *Reduction in Property Costs*

Savings in accommodation costs is a common driver for agile working as it is seen as tangible bottom-line cash saving. There will be a reduction in office space as fewer employees will be working in offices and therefore fewer desks will be required and, through the use of conferencing technologies, there will be reduced demand for meeting and training rooms. The freed accommodation facilities could be repurposed or, where possible, released to reduce cost or raise revenue through renting the surplus accommodation. In cities, the savings in accommodation costs, which include offices, car parking, business rates, service charges, heating, lighting, and maintenance costs, can be considerable. For example in central London, the cost of a desk per person is between £12,000 and £14,000 per annum.

The realization of costs savings from the reduction of accommodation requirements is unlikely to be immediate as the disposal of buildings can take time especially when the activity in the property market is low, or release date in a lease agreement is some time away, and there are contractual restrictions.

### *Reduced Office Relocation Costs*

Moving employees around in traditional offices when organizations restructure departments can be expensive. The costs of internally relocating employees, called "churn costs," can be of the order of £400 per employee moved, as it incurs the refurbishment of offices, for example, erecting or moving partitions. Agile working eliminates these costs, as it is the people that move rather than the facilities.

### *CSR/Sustainability*

Reducing an organization's property space significantly decreases its carbon footprint through a reduction in energy, services, and materials in an office. In addition to the reduction in carbon emissions from the reduced energy usage in the organization's offices, there would be further reductions in the amount of carbon emissions through less business and commuting travel by employees. These reductions in emissions could contribute to the organization's environmental targets. There could also be a reduction in paper and print consumables from the conversion of paper to electronic files.

### *Reduced Employee Attrition*

#### Increased Employee Retention

Agile workers are more likely to stay loyal to an organization offering increased job satisfaction, a modern digital workspace, and improved work–life balance. These organizations will be able to retain their agile workers' skills and knowledge and avoid incurring the considerable costs of recruitment and training new employees. Employees taking maternity or paternity leave will be more likely to return to an organization if they can perform duties in an agile manner.

According to data from Oxford Economics,[2] the average cost of replacing an employee in the UK is around £30,000, with most of this due to lost output while the new employee is brought up to speed. Taking into account the value of a leaving employee's knowledge, reputation,

---

[2] *The Telegraph*. February 2014. "Replacing Employees Costs British Businesses £4bn Each Year." http://telegraph.co.uk/ finance/jobs/10657008/Replacing-employees -costs-British-businesses-4bn-each-year.html

and relationship with clients, some studies[3] put the total cost of losing an employee at 1.5 times an annual salary.

#### More Successful Recruitment

Agile working should enhance an organization's employer brand and help position it as an "employer of choice" enabling it to attract high-quality talent and be more enticing to next-generation workers. The digital workspace enables organizations to manage projects using remote teams so they are no longer limited to local talent and can hire the best talent from anywhere in the world.

#### Increased Diversity in the Workforce

Agile working can be advantageous to those with caring responsibilities (although agile working is not a substitute for child care arrangements) and those with medical problems or disabilities. By offering more agile working arrangements, it should be possible to attract talented employees from people who are no able to work in a traditional office arrangement.

### *Improved Business Continuity*

The traditional approach is to mitigate for the loss of access to the usual place of work or complete loss of premises, through a major incident, is to make contingency provision for office accommodation facilities often contracted from a specialist supplier of a business continuity center. However, these facilities are provided at a considerable "cost per seat," which can be seen as more expensive if the facility is never used. Agile working reduces the requirement of members of the workforce needing to travel to a designated place of work so, in the event of loss of access to buildings, severe weather impacting travel, such as heavy snowfall, or fuel shortages, employees can continue working. So agile working avoids the costs of

---

[3] Alker, J., Editor and Project Lead., M. Malanca, C. Pottage, R. O'Brien. 2016. "Health, Wellbeing & Productivity in Offices." *World Green Building Council.* http:/worldgbc.org/les/6314/1152/0821/WorldGBC__Health_Wellbeing__productivity_Full_Report.pdf

arranging for a business continuity center while making the organization more resilient in the event of a range of incidents such as adverse weather, office fires, and terrorist incidents.

Table 7.1 Lists the top five advantages of agile working cited by recruiters.[4]

*Table 7.1 Top five advantages of agile working cited by recruiters*

| | | |
|---|---|---|
| 1 | Better employee well-being | 68% |
| 2 | Reduced operation costs | 60% |
| 3 | Easier to retain talent | 56% |
| 4 | Attracts better talent | 56% |
| 5 | Flexibility to meet customer demands | 55% |

## The Benefits of Agile Working for Employees

Agile working provides opportunities for people to have a definite improvement in the quality of their life by taking more control of their work activities. Agile working also offers a number of personal benefits for the workforce including:

- Increased choice for employees to manage their work–life balance through greater opportunities to juggle work and nonwork commitments choosing when and where they work.

> *A third (34 percent) of employees would prefer a more flexible approach to working hours than a 3 percent pay rise.*[5]

- Reduced leave sacrificed to deal with domestic events.
- Improved job satisfaction by having clear work objectives and goals, with flexibility in how the targets are achieved.
- A reduction in personal "travel to work" time and associated travel costs through the options of homeworking and other choices of work bases.

[4] Jobsite Survey. November 2017. "Recruiting for the Agile Workforce."

[5] Investors in People's Job Exodus Trends poll 2015.

*The UK Office for National Statistics (ONS) figures show that 3.7 million workers travel for two hours or longer every weekday and this total has increased by a third in five years.*

- Personal productivity by choosing environments with fewer distractions and ready access to colleagues when needed.
- Increase in well-being, health, and happiness, for example, by not being required to work at a designated location and having travel choices to reducing the stress of commuting.

*A major Australian study[6] on 222,000 people aged 45+ found that those that sat down for 11 hours or more each day will increase their risk of dying by 40 percent, over the next three years, regardless of how active they are. The average time spent sitting per day is 9.3 hours, which is more than the average time we spend sleeping at around 7.7 hours.*

Table 7.2 lists the top five advantages of agile working cited by recruitment candidates.[7]

***Table 7.2 Top five advantages of agile working for recruitment candidates***

| Candidate Top 5 | | |
|---|---|---|
| 1 | Better work–life balance | 73% |
| 2 | Flexibility to meet demands | 60% |
| 3 | Better well-being | 54% |
| 4 | Higher productivity | 53% |
| 5 | Less pressure | 39% |

## The Costs of Implementing Agile Working

The benefits of agile working can only be achieved by investing in a number of preparatory activities and resources. A strong business case

[6] Applied Workplace. December 2012. "How to Exercise at Work to Cut Down the Harmful Effects of Sitting."
[7] Jobsite Survey. November 2017. "Recruiting for the Agile Workforce."

will demonstrate that this investment is worthwhile when cost savings and other benefits are established.

The following costs will typically be incurred in an agile working initiative.

### *Surveys*

A space utilization study should be budgeted for to provide detail on how spaces are currently used.

An employee survey of attitudes to agile working may also incur costs.

### *Premises*

Most agile working initiatives result in a reduction of premises, but there may be additional property costs (e.g., for lease, business rates, heating, lighting, and ventilation) if the organization is relocating offices to a new location that may be offset by the costs saved by releasing the previous premises. However, increased utilization of the premises may lead to an increase in occupancy costs such as heating, lighting, and ventilation.

### *Furniture*

Agile working requires the provision of a range of furniture that supports more varied work locations and will include desks/workstations, booths, pods, lockers, chairs, soft seating, and furniture for formal and informal meeting rooms. Agile working requires quality furniture so that employees will want to use the spaces you create.

Allowance should also be made for the fees of a specialist designer of agile working environments along with the purchase, delivery, and installation of new furniture, and the removal of any old furniture.

### *Technology*

There is likely to be a number of technology-related costs:

- It may be necessary to upgrade specific IT systems to enable them to support agile working and acquire new infrastructure, for example, the acquisition of Unified Communications.

- Agile workers will need to be equipped with suitable devices such as laptops, tablets, and also headsets.
- Meeting rooms may need upgrading with smart boards on other screen-based equipment for displaying information to groups of people.
- Software licenses are likely to be required for conferencing and collaboration tools although some are bundled into general office software.
- There will also be license costs for a system for booking rooms and shared desks and other shared facilities.

### *Program Team*

An agile working program will require a substantial team from a range of disciplines (see Chapter 9). Some of these roles will require the contracting of specialist consultants and even when it is intended that internal employees will be used that should not be regarded as a free resource and an estimate of the opportunity costs of dedicating them to the program should be made.

### *Training*

A program of facilitated workshops and training as described in Chapter 10 will need to be costed.

## Workstyle Analysis

Workstyle analysis is a crucial component in the preparation for the adoption of agile working and will help to inform the business case. The workstyles, or ways of working categories, as described in Chapter 2, are usually categorized by job role and the locations where the jobholder carries out their work activities. For each of the categories, the work settings and technology requirements can be determined. With an estimate of how many employees are assigned to each workstyle the cost of providing these facilities can be estimated for the business case using agility ratios. An agility ratio is merely the number of people allocated to the number of

desks (or how many desks are required to accommodate a given number of people).

In traditional offices, every employee is allocated a desk, so the agility ratio is 1:1. In fact this is usually an overgenerous agility ratio, as after allowing for holidays, illness, and employees attending meetings and training courses an agility ratio of 8 desks for 10 employees is usually sufficient if the allocation of desks is flexible. In agile working there is scope to reduce further the number of desks provided as agile workers, enabled by developments in mobile technology, generally, spend less time at a designated desk. There will be a range of new ways of working from this that have a high degree of autonomy and mobility to those that are required to work at a number of defined locations and some that still work at designated single "fixed desk." However, the categorizing of employees, typically those in customer-facing roles as needing a fixed desk workstyle, should be challenged. For example, as described in Chapter 5, receptionists do not need to be sat at fixed front desk, small businesses, who cannot afford a full-time receptionist, often provide a call button system, sometimes supported by CCTV, to alert employees who can take on the receptionist role to greet visitors via an intercom. Many call center employees can be home-based.

It is not feasible to define a personal workstyle for every employee, but it is possible to categorize employees to a manageable number (typically no more than six) of workstyles based principally on the locations where they undertake their work tasks.

H22

The purpose of workstyle analysis is to understand better the ways of working and the space, technology, and facilities required of employees categorized by each workstyle. In developing the business case, workstyle analysis can estimate the costs of providing these facilities for agile workers in each category and also the savings from the reduction of accommodation resulting from lower agility ratios.

The physical and technology requirements of the typical workstyles listed in Chapter 2 are described below.

- **Fixed desk employees** work at the same position in their base and, for business or occupational health reasons, have little or no opportunity to work at other locations. They typically would have the use of a desk within a single location, using a desktop computer and a locker for personal storage. Their agility ratio will be 1:1 but when not present for extended periods of time (e.g., more than a half day) they should accept that others might use their work setting.

- **Fixed location employees** work in various work settings in a shared team area in one of the buildings owned or leased by the organization. They typically would have the use of a group of work settings within a designated team area, and allocated on an agreed "person to desk ratio." Each desk should be equipped with similar workstations often Thin Client computers[8] and universal connectivity. Individual lockers would be provided for each employee within the team area. The agility ratio for fixed location employees will be less than fixed desk employees.
- **Multi-site employees** work in various work settings around their base and also regularly in other premises of the organization. They would have a similar equipment provision to fixed location, using a room and desk booking system to ensure access to traditional workspaces when required, or utilizing "touchdown" spaces provided within appropriate team areas on the organization's premises. They could use their personal computer at home provided it is equipped with client software, such as Citrix Receiver, to access applications hosted on remote servers. Lockers would be provided for temporary use. The agility ratio for multi-site employees is likely to be similar to fixed location employees.
- **Nomadic employees** work for the majority of their time remote from their base, in other premises of the organization, at its partner's premises, in the community, and at home. They are often described as mobile workers but will enjoy a high degree of autonomy. These employees would work across the geographical area of their responsibility, using a

[8] A thin client is a desktop terminal that has no hard drive. All features typically found on the desktop PC, including applications, data, memory, and so on, are stored in a data center or the Cloud. Thin client technology also allows users to log into their home computer.

room and desk booking system or utilizing "**"touchdown**" spaces provided within relevant team areas at offices and other facilities (including partner spaces). They would be expected to work regularly at home or third-party premises, except when security or other issues restrict such practice. Employees in this workstyle may be issued with laptop computers so the work settings would need to provide some form of a docking station (i.e., screens and keyboards) to support these devices. They could use their personal computer at home.

- **Contractual home-based employees** carry out the majority of tasks at home with attendance at the premises of the organization only required for the occasional team and supervisory meetings. Employers may choose to provide a high-quality network connection and secure filing and scanning facilities (where security requirements permit). When required to attend the employer organization premises they would make use of the facilities available to employees with nomadic workstyle.

For each designated workstyle it is possible to devise a technology "package" (comprising computers, mobile devices, and software tools) and a facilities package (comprising workstations and personal storage). The amount of equipment required can be calculated using agreed agility ratios, and the cost of their provision can be estimated. Table 7.3 illustrates a possible set of packages associated with the sample workstyles.

*Table 7.3 Proposed workstyle environments*

| | Fixed desk | Fixed location | Multi-site | Nomadic | Contractual home |
|---|---|---|---|---|---|
| **Physical workspace** | Dedicated desk | Shared desks | Shared desks and touchdown desks | Shared desks and touchdown desks | Home and touchdown desks |
| **Equipment** | Desktop PC | Thin client PC | Thin client PC | Laptop computers | Thin client PC |
| **Homeworking?** | Not expected | Not expected | Occasionally | Regular place of work | Normal place of work |

*As organizations pursue agile working and the digital workspace the proportion of employees with a nomadic workstyle will increase and is likely to be the predominant workstyle.*

## Using Options Appraisal

In practice, there will be more than one way that agile working can be implemented so the business case should include an "options appraisal." In this process a number of potential options would be evaluated in terms of costs and benefits and a preferred course of action established. There should be a "do nothing" option, which is the continuation of the current way of working, and this can provide a benchmark for the comparison of the alternatives.

As an example, the categorization of the options could be cautious, moderate, and ambitious representing the degree of change from current working practices. These options could be further subdivided by different combinations of the investment in technologies (e.g., thin client or laptops), facilities, and furniture (e.g., whether to purchase new furniture or repurpose existing furniture). The options should be distinct and based on factors relevant to the organization.

### *Payback Period*

The options could be differentiated by their payback period. The payback period is the length of time required to recover the cost of an investment, or "break even." It looks at the cumulative costs and savings over a period of time, typically a number of years for agile working. In general, shorter payback periods are preferable to longer payback periods. So in Figure 7.2 Scenario 1 is the preferred option.

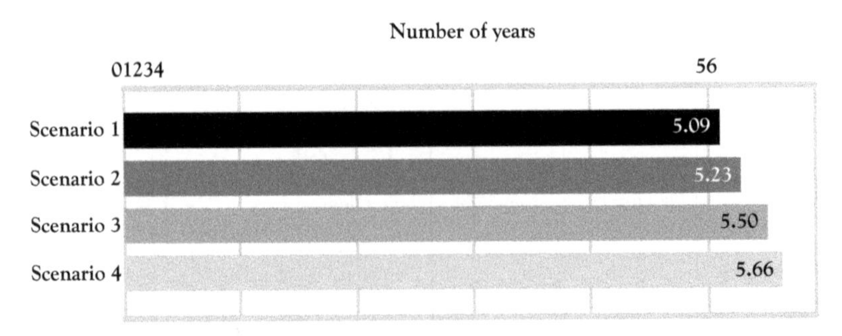


*Figure 7.2 Payback periods*

However agile working is not just about financial returns, and the returns of other objectives need to be weighed in. Some of these objectives may not be cashable such as improved customer services or promote the organization's corporate social responsibility. The preferred option should be chosen after all the relevant factors have been considered and prioritized.

### *Benefit Realization Plan*

Once the preferred option is chosen, and the business benefits have been confirmed, it is important to set up a mechanism with metrics to track the benefits and check they are realized during or after the implementation of agile working. A table can be set up to track the benefits. The table should contain:

- The benefit desired
- Description of the benefit
- Type of benefit (e.g., cash saving, productivity, or quality improvement)
- How the benefit will be measured—this may require evidence from employees or space utilization surveys
- The person responsible for evaluating the benefit
- The target date when benefit should be realized—this will be indicative initially and revised when a program plan has been agreed

*In reality, many programs are kicked off without a business case, but I would argue that a business case, at an appropriate level of detail, will provide an essential reference point to remind everyone of the objectives and the benefits of the program when the going gets tough. In constructing the business case, it is best to take an organizationwide view to identify areas where agile working could best increase effectiveness and meet the strategic aims of the organization. This view should be tempered with a realistic assessment of business readiness for new ways of working.*

# CHAPTER 8

# Developing an Agile Working Strategy

The agile working strategy should have a particular focus on cultural change. There will need to be an emphasis on engagement to develop a culture for agile working. People will need to feel that they can contribute their own ideas and will be informed and supported during the transition to new ways of working.

## Vision

The vision should describe the future state of agile working and the digital workspace and how it will benefit all stakeholders. The agile working vision should involve a "dialogue" with employees including those who are favorable to new ways of working and those who are not. While it may take time to formulate and agree, the vision should be the result of collaboration with key parties to build a consensus. The vision should be consistent with the organization's values and serve as a source of inspiration to the stakeholders so they will adopt the strategy and help realize the vision. It is useful to provide a personalized vision, such as "a day in the life," so that employees can understand how the new way of working will affect them and how it can enhance their working experience.

An agile working vision should be enterprisewide and include all employees. Otherwise, some employees will feel excluded and alienated. It should also relate to the organization's business goals that the organization hopes to realize through the agile working and digital workspace initiative, for example, changing the culture by breaking down silos and improving communication and collaboration, enhancing performance, reducing costs, and so on.

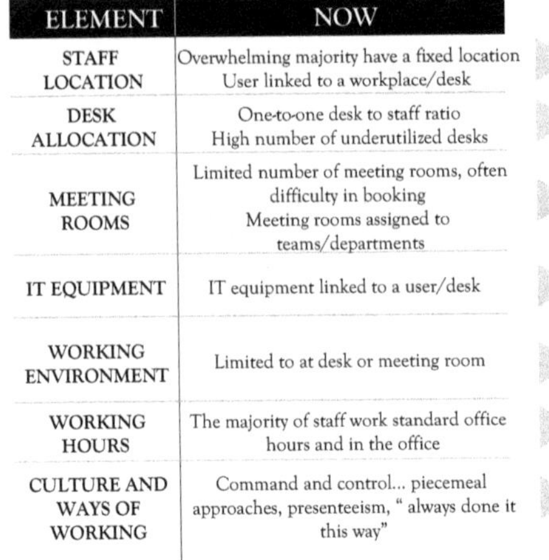

| ELEMENT | NOW | FUTURE |
|---|---|---|
| STAFF LOCATION | Overwhelming majority have a fixed location<br>User linked to a workplace/desk | Flexible location for as many people as possible including home and distributed locations |
| DESK ALLOCATION | One-to-one desk to staff ratio<br>High number of underutilized desks | Reduce desk to staff ratio<br>Based on evidence and business need |
| MEETING ROOMS | Limited number of meeting rooms, often difficulty in booking<br>Meeting rooms assigned to teams/departments | Alternative activity-based settings and shared collaborativespaces, reducing the need for meeting rooms, but increasing the availability of meeting space |
| IT EQUIPMENT | IT equipment linked to a user/desk | Focus on screen-based working<br>Unified Comms. platform, and support |
| WORKING ENVIRONMENT | Limited to at desk or meeting room | Work activity zones enabling staff to choose the environment that best suits their work<br>Support to remote workers |
| WORKING HOURS | The majority of staff work standard office hours and in the office | Business-focused flexible working enabling work life blend |
| CULTURE AND WAYS OF WORKING | Command and control... piecemeal approaches, presenteeism, " always done it this way" | Framework for personal empowerment, coaching and mentoring, focus on work outcomes, open to innovation, involving everyone |

*Figure 8.1 An agile transformation*

Figure 8.1 illustrates how a vision could be interpreted by comparing the future with the current ways of working.

## Strategic Aims

No two agile working and digital workspace strategies will be identical and will depend on the intended objectives and outcomes. These are some examples of the strategic aims organizations have chosen:

- To create a more responsive, efficient, and effective organization, which improves business performance and increases customer satisfaction.
- To provide a healthy workplace and good work–life balance for employees.
- To provide an environment that encourages innovation and celebrates success.
- To provide a motivated, high-performing, and empowered workforce.
- To create an environment where the focus is on the quality of work rather than where it is produced.
- To unlock the savings associated with property strategy by adopting an agile working model.

- To encourage and improve information sharing and the collaboration between teams.
- To maximize the use of investment in technology.

## The Need for a Holistic Approach

Experience with organizations that have successfully introduced new ways of working indicates that a holistic approach is required to achieve the strategic objectives.

The successful implementation of any new ways of working requires an integrated approach involving the people, property, technology, and security functions to support the operational needs of the organization. Figure 8.2 shows the departments likely to have a vital role in the implementation of agile working.

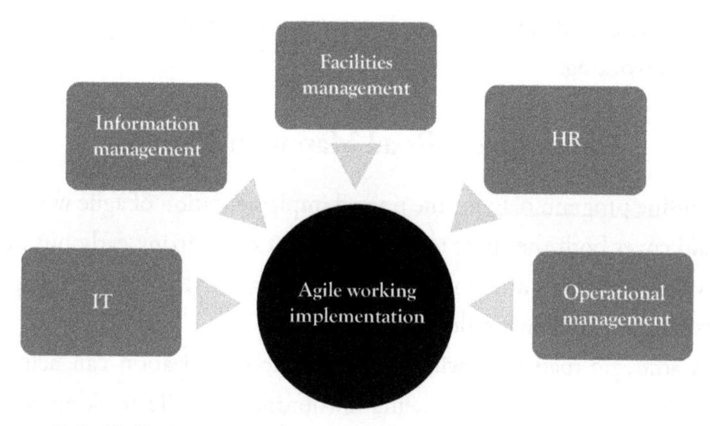


*Figure 8.2 Holistic approach*

Bringing together information management, IT/technology, estates, security, HR, and operational management initiatives in to a single overarching agile working program will ensure that all the necessary elements are in place for the successful rollout of agile working across the organization.

The establishment of an agile working program should be regarded as an opportunity to coordinate the interdependencies of major projects, such as:

- Business transformation
- Digitalization

- New accommodation initiatives
- Well-being and other HR initiatives

The establishment of an agile working program with prioritization and alignment with related projects should ensure that the realization of the benefits of all the initiatives is maximized.

This holistic approach should ensure that:

- The technologies and systems are ready as agile working is rolled out.
- The accommodation and work settings are in place.
- Digitalization initiatives are aligned with agile working implementation.
- Employees are prepared to work differently through timely communications, learning, engagement, and leadership.
- Policies and guidelines are in place to support new ways of working.

## Developing a Road Map with Phasing

An outline program plan for the phased implementation of agile working should cover both the short term (focused on maximizing early business value, "quick wins") and longer term including activities to sustain agile working post-implementation.

A strategic road map will show how the organization can achieve its business goals. The implementation journey of agile working could proceed in the four phases as illustrated in Figure 8.3.

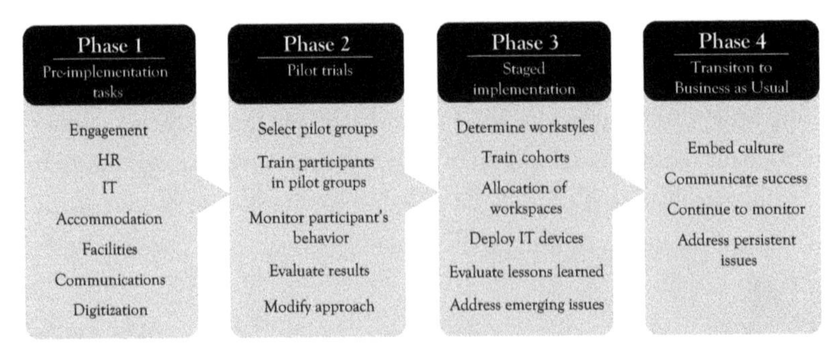


***Figure 8.3 The four phases of the agile working implementation road map***

### *Phase 1: Pre-Implementation Activities*

The enabling departments such as information management, IT/technology, estates, security, and HR will need to undertake a number of activities (as described in Chapter 10) to put in place measures prior to the implementation of agile working.

### *Phase 2: Pilot Trials*

A "big bang" approach to implementing agile working heightens the risks of what is likely to be a challenging program. It is better to test the intended approach by running small-scale pilots. A pilot provides an opportunity to gather detailed feedback, evaluate, and make changes as required.

Before the full-scale implementation of the agile working program, a number of pilot trials should be conducted to ensure that the approach is appropriate, serviceable, and robust in concept. In this way, any shortcomings or elements of the solutions proposed can be identified and the approach modified.

The pilot trials could be conducted in two stages:

1. An alpha trial to demonstrate the proof of concept. For this trial, it may be better to choose a function or department that is explicitly supportive of the initiative and willing to be accepting if deficiencies are discovered that need to be addressed.
2. A beta trial has a very different purpose, which is to provide convincing evidence for the adoption of agile working throughout the organization. Unlike the alpha trial, the departments of the organization that should be invited to participate in the beta trials should have no vested interests in promoting the solution and be neutral, or even slightly antagonistic, to the initiative so the results can be seen as independent. The selection of participants should be based on clear criteria to ensure that the success of the pilot trail can be established. Criteria could include:

    - There is a demonstrable benefit in moving to a new way of working.

- The groups chosen are resilient enough not to affect adversely any major service delivery capability of the organization.
- The teams have the opportunity to adopt new ways of working.
- There are practical elements of change in their environment—new work settings/work practices/technology.
- Participants are willing to share their successful experiences.

The trials should be set up to test:

- the effectiveness of the steps in the implementation plan
- the allocation of workstyles
- the method of allocating IT and facilities
- the appropriateness of the agility ratios
- the accommodation's support infrastructures
- the effectiveness of the training

Where possible the trial should include the use of partner premises and other "third party places" to test the feasibility of their use by employees with more mobile workstyles.

Ideally, the participants should be able to receive all elements of the program as an entirety, so that the performance of the overall solution can be assessed. However, there may be a number of reasons why this may not be possible, for example, the new accommodation or new IT facilities may not yet be in place, in which case trials will need to take account of the state of "Agile Working Readiness" of some functions. For these trial groups, there may be only limited benefits from the trial.

The trials will provide an opportunity to gather evidence and feedback from the participants. Once the initial testing has taken place, there should be a review to identify successes and any critical shortcomings. Lessons learned may need to be incorporated into a revised business case and strategy. The results of the pilot trials should be communicated in a constructive way. If there are elements that have not proved as effective as anticipated there may be a need for further trials to test if remedial actions are effective.

### *Phase 3: Staged Implementation*

The rollout of the agile working program should be aligned with other projects on which it is dependent.

Figure 8.4 presents a suggested framework for a phased implementation by departments based on agile working readiness and size (expressed as numbers of employees).

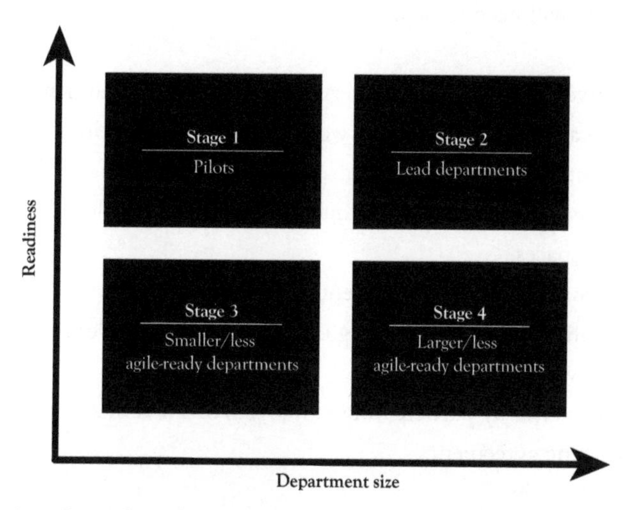


*Figure 8.4 Staged implementation*

Provisional candidate departments for the four phases of implementation could be identified as follows:

**Stage 1:** The departments in the upper left quadrant (low employee numbers but high state of readiness) could be considered as candidates for pilot trials of agile working. Ideally a variety of departments should be trialed.

**Stage 2:** The departments in the upper right quadrant (high employee numbers and high state of readiness) can be considered as lead candidates for the first rollout of the agile working program.

**Stage 3:** The departments in the lower left quadrant (low employee numbers and low state of readiness) can be considered for the third phase of the agile working program.

**Stage 4:** The departments in the lower right quadrant (high employee numbers but low state of readiness) can be considered for the remaining phase of the agile working program and as a consequence will have more time to prepare for the transition to the new way of working.

Prior to the implementation of each stage of the program, the following activities will need to be undertaken:

- Conversion of relevant paper files to electronic documents
- Allocation of employees to workstyles as described in Chapter 7
- Provision of shared desks, touchdown areas, and allocation of workspaces
- Procurement and deployment of devices
- Familiarization and learning of managers and employees in agile working
- Acceptance by participating employees of the terms of an agile working agreement

After each stage of the implementation there should be:

- An evaluation of the lessons learned from implementation
- An assessment of the benefits realized
- A consideration of the future development of elements in the agile working journey

Provision should be made to measure the key performance indicators (KPIs), based on the business objectives, before and after the implementation, to quantify the impact of the implementation.

### *Phase 4: Longer-Term Transition to Business as Usual*

The embedding of agile working as the preferred way of working will extend beyond the implementation program. Therefore in Phase 4 the initiative will move from a program basis to a sustainable "Business as Usual" model that continues to develop as technology and accommodation provision evolves. The measures to be included in Phase 4 are discussed in Chapter 12.

# CHAPTER 9

# Setting up an Agile Working Program

Flexible working has been with us since the beginning of the millennium, and there are plenty of qualified project managers around, over one million people have taken the PRINCE2 certification since it was established in 1996. So introducing an agile working program should be easy, right? Wrong.

Agile working is more challenging than flexible working, and most business transformation programs, in that it seeks behavior change of employees beyond their (increasingly notional) nine-to-five working hours and impacts, some would say threatens, the life component of their work–life balance.

For a successful implementation of agile working some initial program activities will need to be put in place:

- Setting up governance
- The appointment of a program manager, program board, and confirmation of the program governance model
- Development of a Program Communications and Engagement Plan

## Governance

*Good governance is like having good brakes on the car it makes it safer to go faster*

—Ralph O'Brien

An active program board is a vital ingredient in successful program governance. The principal activities of the program board include:

- authorizing initiation;
- authorizing a program;
- providing ad hoc direction; and
- confirming the closure of the program.

*Note: In this book the agile working initiative is assumed to be managed as a program as it would be a major initiative comprising a number of projects for accommodation, technology, culture change, and so on. For a smaller implementation of agile working the initiative could be managed as a project with constituent workstreams. However, the same general principles apply to both an agile working program and a project.*

Figure 9.1 shows the typical members of an agile working program board. It is essential that the right people with the appropriate skills, knowledge, and experience are selected for the program board.

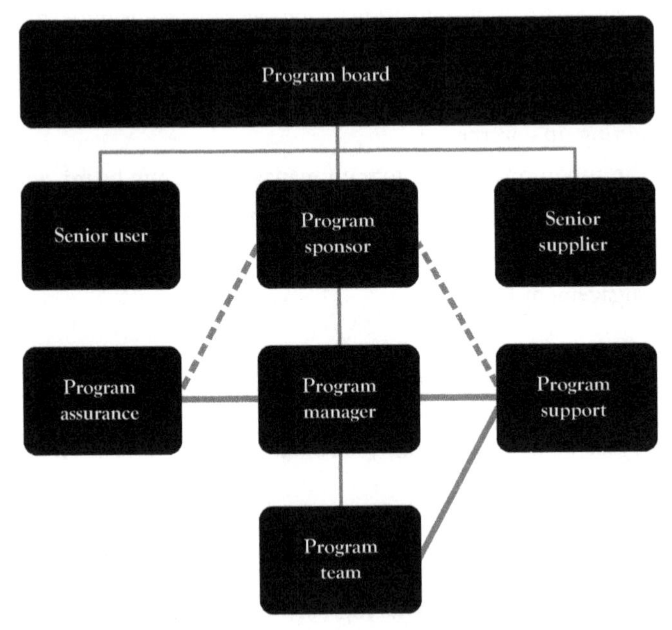


***Figure 9.1 An agile working program board***

The three critical roles for agile working programs are the program sponsor, senior user(s), and program manager.

### *Program Sponsor*

The principal responsibilities of the program sponsor are first to identify the need for the program and define it at a high level. Secondly, the program sponsor is responsible for the program's business case and should not hesitate to recommend cancelation of the program if the business case no longer justifies the program. The program sponsor should set up and chair the program board. While the program board authorizes the major program decisions, an essential role of the program sponsor is to maintain the progress of the program by making executive decisions between program board meetings. The sponsor's decisions can be reported and ratified at the next program board meeting.

One of the most serious problems for any program is not having the right person as the program sponsor. The sponsor needs the appropriate authority, but they should also have sufficient time to commit to their role. The sponsor is usually an executive or member of management and champions the program, and holds the program budget. A board-level program sponsor can ensure that sufficient resources are made available to the program and that senior management understand the business benefits of the program.

Agile working will impact many activities of the organization and is likely to be resisted by some managers. Further impetus can be gained by setting up a network of empowered business champions across different functions of the organization. Business champions should voluntarily promote the adoption of agile working and will seek to overcome any entrenched internal resistance to change on the part of the organization they represent.

### *Senior User*

The senior user represents the operational functions of the organization that will adopt the new ways of working to achieve the objectives or obtain the business benefits. This role is often a make-or-break element in the program's governance. The active involvement of leaders and managers as senior users will be critical to the success of the program.

The commitment of the senior user is vital. Senior managers will have many demands on their time. While they may be supportive of the program, they may not be able to afford it sufficient priority over day-to-day demands, and they may choose not to attend program board meetings. While these absences can be overcome if well-briefed deputies attend in their place, this is usually a second-best option and risks a loss of continuity in decision making.

Staff from user departments will be a critical resource for an agile working program, as they provide the pool of candidates to be agile workers and will need to be supported by their line managers. In turn, their managers need the support and encouragement of the senior user who should also represent their concerns at the program board. These employees will also have "day jobs" and their time will need to be freed up on the authority of the senior user otherwise the program could stall.

### *Agile Working Program Manager*

The agile working program should be led by a program manager supported by, as well as accountable to, the program board. Agile working is a logistical undertaking, which requires the overall control of a single person responsible for overseeing the delivery of the program. A dedicated program manager will coordinate the cross-disciplinary core team of people brought together from the different support areas of the organization.

The primary responsibilities of the agile working program manager include:

- Ensuring that the program maintains its alignment with the strategic objectives of the organization.
- Determining priorities and allocating human and financial resources in line with the priorities.
- Developing and managing the program plan in conjunction with the workstream leads.
- Monitoring and coordinating the supporting projects and supervising their implementation.

- Assessing the risks and issues of the program and creating action plans to mitigate those risks.
- Reporting and communicating program activity and progress.

Agile working requires a particular sort of program manager who is happy to deal with the fuzzy outcomes of behavioral change. Program managers who are most comfortable with the mechanics of detailed program plans and product breakdown structures may find the subtleties of an agile working initiative unsettling.

### *Other Roles Required for the Agile Working program.*

The following roles are recommended for the agile working program.

**Program Team:** The program team should comprise employees seconded for enabling departments, for example, IT, HR, estates, and information management. Ideally, these team members would have this responsibility as part of their primary responsibility, but it may be one component of a range of duties that they will be performing for the organization. The program team should include dedicated communications manager and change manager to ensure a successful transformation.

**The Senior Supplier:** The senior suppliers' role represents those who will design, develop, facilitate, procure, and implement the program's products likely to be technology, furniture, and facilities. There may be more than one external senior supplier, for example, one for the supply and fitting furniture and equipment and another for the supply and installation of technology.

Problems can arise if the senior supplier has not devoted sufficient resources to their tasks or they extend themselves beyond their employees' competencies. Technical issues that are unexpected and difficult to identify and resolve can send the program off track. The other members of the project board may not have the technical knowledge to understand the nature of the issues and can feel frustrated by delays.

**Technical Assurance:** This role is responsible for the technical integrity of the program.

**Program Management Office:** A project management office provides a central support service to the program: creating and maintaining documentation, recording the program's metrics, and regularly monitoring performance.

## Identifying Stakeholders

The group of stakeholders in agile working programs is potentially wide-ranging, for example, there are likely to be HR and legal issues arising in the program. While the communications program will be needed to brief managers and employees, all interested and impacted groups should be identified through a careful stakeholder analysis. The organization should consider a "brand identity" for the program to highlight the initiative.

Outside of the formal members of the program board, there will be other key stakeholders such as:

- Senior leadership team
- Trade unions and other bodies representing employees
- Regulators
- Parent company
- Board members

## Developing a Program Plan

An indicative program plan with milestones should be developed to help establish timescales and resources. The plan will need to be refined so that a highly detailed Gantt chart illustrating every step of the program can be prepared. The chart should highlight lead-in times for major items that will need to be procured such as IT systems and specialist furniture.

To be manageable, the agile working program plan should be broken down into a number of workstreams. The dependencies of the workstreams and related projects should be established so that the impact of delays or changes in a workstream on the overall program can be monitored. For example, a project to convert paper documents to electronic files is often a key dependency for the implementation of agile working.

## Addressing the Technical Aspects of Program Management

### *Scope*

Many people find agile working challenging to define, so there should be clarity as to what is included in the agile working program and what isn't. A fuzzy definition will make it difficult to attribute business benefits, while an unfocused program team is a recipe for failure.

### *Identifying Risks and Their Mitigation*

It is good project management practice to establish a register of risks associated with new ways of working, how they will be mitigated, and who is responsible for resolving them. A range of risks is likely to be identified in the agile working business case; other risks will emerge as the agile working program is implemented. A risk register (see Table 9.1) should be set up and maintained by the program manager and reviewed on a regular basis by the program board.

The most significant risks in an agile working program usually relate to lack of management and employees buy-in. Other common examples are:

- Lack of leadership by senior management
- Delay in office moves
- Delay in IT provision
- Performance of IT and systems off-premise not adequate
- Reduction in employee performance
- Data breaches

### *Issues log*

In an agile working program, it is difficult to envisage all the likely people and technical issues at the outset. An issue log (see Table 9.2) should be set up and maintained throughout the program. Issues should be documented and allocated to a member of the program team to resolve, and their resolution should be actively monitored.

*Table 9.1 Risk register template*

| Risk | Probability High/medium/low | Impact High/medium/low | Mitigation | Risk owner |
|---|---|---|---|---|
| 1. | | | | |
| 2. | | | | |
| 3. | | | | |
| 4. | | | | |
| 5. | | | | |
| 6. | | | | |
| 7. | | | | |
| 8. | | | | |

*Table 9.2* ***Issue log template***

| ID | Date raised | Issue | Owner | Action | Type | Severity | Status |
|---|---|---|---|---|---|---|---|
| 1. | | | | | | | |
| 2. | | | | | | | |
| 3. | | | | | | | |
| 4. | | | | | | | |
| 5. | | | | | | | |
| 6. | | | | | | | |
| 7. | | | | | | | |
| 8. | | | | | | | |

To prevent scope creep, the inclusion of significant issues should be formally approved as the amendments to the program documentation through a change control process.

### *Highlight Reports*

For any transformational program, regular progress reports, in the form of highlight reports, will help to continue to engage the stakeholders. Some stakeholders are likely to be highly skeptical, and news of positive progress will help counter doubt and assure the program board of the program's continuing viability. Regular highlight reports will also alert the program board to new issues and risks so that they can deal with them in a timely manner. The highlight report should contain

- Project status
- Activities completed for the reporting period
- Activities planned for next reporting period
- New dependencies/impacts
- New/outstanding issues
- Decisions required
- Decisions taken
- Actions outstanding
- Change requests
- Updated program plan

## Benefits Realization and Evaluation of the Program

It is important to measure the success of the program against the goals set out in the business case. Business benefits identified in the preparation of the business case for agile working should be tracked and quantified as described in Chapter 7. The realization of business benefits will provide evidence that the agile working strategy has achieved its predicted outcomes. However, it should be recognized that some of the benefits may not be realized until some months after the implementation of the agile working program is complete as employees may need time to adopt new ways of working.

To measure progress during the program's implementation, it should be possible to set up metrics for key performance indicators (KPIs) as the implementation is progressing such as:

- Workforce effectiveness
- Employee agility
- Employee satisfaction
- Employee retention

Relevant metrics can provide a valuable feedback mechanism for the continuous development of the agile working strategy, and serve as useful tools for change management.

These KPIs could be assessed by using:

- An employees' opinion survey to see how your employees are getting on with the new space
- Post-occupancy utilization studies to measure the take up of the facilities
- A more detailed observation study to see how different areas are being used

It is also important to track the effectiveness of the agile working program itself so that changes can be made to later phases of the program. Each phase of the agile working program should provide a valuable learning experience.

The evaluation of the agile working program can take two forms:

1. "Lessons-learned" reviews held by the program team at the end of each stage of the program, say every three or four months. These reviews should be focused on how well the program is being, or has been, delivered. People at every level of the organization should be given an opportunity to share their insights.
2. A post-implementation review (PIR) should be conducted sometime after the program, or a significant phase, of the program, has finished and new ways of working have been adopted. The PIR will typically consider:

- Has the program achieved its intended objectives?
- Have changes in behavior been achieved?
- Have business benefits been realized?

## Why Agile Working Initiatives Can Fail

The business case is signed off; the agile working program has the backing of senior management, what could possibly go wrong? Well plenty, unfortunately. While few agile working initiatives fail spectacularly many do not realize the business benefits envisaged.

Almost all the press coverage on agile working has invariably been positive, and there have been a number of significant success stories. But to assume an agile working initiative will always be successfully implemented and easily sustained is unrealistic. So what are the problems?

Not getting the governance right. Too often an agile working program is made the responsibility of just one department in an organization, such as property, HR, or IT. A single department will not have the knowledge or resources to address all the people, technology, and workplace factors that need to be addressed in a successful implementation of agile working. The head of a single department may also lack the "clout" to get the cooperation of the other enabling departments. A further error is not consulting the operational managers of the business functions and service departments when the agile working strategy is being formulated.

Technology can be critical to the success or failure of an agile working initiative. IT systems may not perform well when accessed remotely, and the infrastructure, both data and voice, may not provide reliable connections in all areas that people choose or need to work. Agile workers may not be confident when using collaborative tools when away from an office environment, where colleagues are not on hand to help or when working outside the normal working hours when the IT helpdesk is closed. People are becoming increasingly sensitive to the equipment they are required to use when out and about. A one-size-fits-all approach to the issue of devices to employees may prove unpopular, for example, common complaints are that laptops are too heavy or their screens are too small for practical use for the job role.

Agile working in the office can also be problematic. Office work settings may be inappropriate. In some cases, an organization's agile working initiative is not much more than setting up a hotdesk area with little thought as to how it will be used. For example, where there are no protocols on how to take phone calls without distracting colleagues, the resulting noisy environment will be a cause of exasperation.

The additional facilities needed to support the range of work activities—creative, collaborative, and contemplative—may not have been considered or the numbers of these facilities not correctly estimated. The use of cheap, inappropriate furniture will only exacerbate the situation.

However, the most common problems relate to employees' attitudes to agile working. People may not feel engaged if they have not been consulted when the implementation is planned, and regard agile working as merely a cost-cutting exercise and feel exploited, as they see no benefits for themselves.

Even when people have enthusiastically bought into the agile working initiative with high expectations, if there is a lack of continuing communication and/or progress, their initial excitement may subside and turn into disenchantment. Regardless of their attitude to the initiative employees may have anxieties. Many employees can become uneasy when they realize that they are no longer sharing an office with team members they are used to seeing every day. In light of these situations, the promised improvements in productivity in the agile working business case may prove elusive.

The group of employees most likely to push back on agile working is middle management. Operational middle managers often feel they are the "meat in the sandwich." They are urged to embrace new ways of working by the senior management while dealing with high expectations of an improved work–life balance of the people they manage. Worse still they are expected to continue to meet their targets while managing employees, who are no longer visible to them, in ways that are alien to them. To be fair, managing by results, that is, assessing outputs in terms of the quality of work done, is a great deal more challenging than using input measures such as hours worked in the office. This group of managers may find that, for them, the glib slogan, "work smarter not harder," is reversed.

# CHAPTER 10

# Implementing Agile Working

To be manageable, the agile working program should be broken down into a number of workstreams:

- Engagement and culture change
- HR
- Technology
- Accommodation
- Facilities
- Learning and ongoing support

Within these workstreams, there are a number of activities that will need to be undertaken prior to the implementation of agile working.

## Communications and Engagement

Successful agile working results from changes in employee behavior and cannot be dictated by policy but through a program of personal communication and engagement will employees voluntarily commit to agile working. When employees understand and appreciate the reasons behind the new way of working, explained in a way that is relevant to them and their teams, they are far more likely to support it.

A key factor for the successful implementation of agile working is clear communication, giving people an understanding of why the organization is adopting a new way of working. There is now a wide range of communication styles and technologies available to use, including social media, blogs, videos, intranets, e-mails, frequently asked questions (FAQs), online forums, workshops, newsletters, posters, and so on. However, it is important that everyone involved in the program is able and willing to use the communications technologies effectively. Also important is identifying the key messages and the frequency of communications for each of the defined audiences.

*Quantitative data may make an overwhelming business case, but anecdotal evidence may be needed to sway hearts and minds. Providing a narrative supported by real-life experiences will help sell the concepts and principles of new ways of working.*

The components of the agile working engagement and communication plan should include:

- Identification of the agile working program stakeholders and audiences, who should be engaged early and often.
- A simple articulation of the benefits for each identified audience.
- Case studies relevant to the organization, the users of its services, and individual members of the workforce alike.
- A before and after "a day in the life" scenario can be a very persuasive way to show how employees will benefit from new ways of working.
- Program branding and communication templates.
- Providing employees with a channel to give feedback.
- Developing and managing employee surveys and publishing their outcomes.
- Managing external public relations and related communications for the program.

It is important to provide regular communications before (to prepare employees), during (to encourage), and after (to reinforce behaviors) the implementation of agile working.

## HR

HR will have a central role in the preparation for the implementation of agile working and the effect it will have on employees. HR will have the practical tasks of reviewing HR policies and employment contracts to ensure they are supportive of agile working.

### *Revision of Current HR Policies*

Table 10.1 suggests the HR policies and procedures that may need to be reviewed and adapted to ensure that they support the new ways of working. An overarching agile working policy could be developed to define employer and employee responsibilities for the new ways of working. This policy will need to take into account any statutory rights, for example, for employees to request flexible working.

The creation of new policies should be avoided, wherever possible. The aim should be to reinforce still relevant policies and seek to reduce the number of existing procedures and replace them with a smaller number of guidelines that reflect the autonomy afforded to agile workers.

***Table 10.1 HR policies for review***

| | |
|---|---|
| Appraisal | Learning and development |
| Contractors | Management development |
| Contract variation | Performance management |
| Disciplinary | Personal safety and lone working |
| Employee consultation | Probationary period and trainees |
| Employer insurance policies | Promotion |
| Equality and diversity | Recruitment and selection |
| Financial authority and ordering process | Redundancy and redeployment |
| Flexible working, including caring leave | Relocation |
| Grievance | Secondment |
| Health and safety | Sickness absence |
| Homeworking | Stress at work |
| Induction and probation | Travel expenses |
| Job-sharing | Working hours and time-recording |

A possibly contentious area is the policies that relate to homeworking. Agile working requires clear rules, so employees are sure of their responsibilities and opportunities for homeworking. There is an essential difference between those who are contractually based homeworkers, that is, their home is their designated place of work and they only visit their employer's premises for specific business reasons, and all other employees who work at home.

Other types of homeworkers are:

- **Regular homeworkers**—those that have an agreement with their employer to work at home for a number of days per week, per month, or certain times of the year.
- **Occasional homeworkers**—those that have less formal arrangements to work at home, for example, to finish writing a report.
- **"Day extenders"**—those that work beyond their "official" working day, for example, sending e-mails in evenings, finishing reports at weekends. This way of working is often an unrecognized form of homeworking, but these employees should still be subject to the organization's homeworking policies, especially those that relate to security as described below.

Depending on national legislation it is likely that employees working at home will be required to affirm they have a safe and suitable place to work at home. However, with the advent of ubiquitous Wi-Fi, it is possible to work in a variety of locations including the garden (if the sun is not shining too brightly!).

### *Review of Employment Contracts*

Employee contracts should be reviewed to ensure there are no restrictions that would inhibit designated employees from adopting agile working. Contractually based homeworkers will need specific contractual arrangements, for example, they would be able to claim travel expenses when traveling to their employer's offices and may be provided with equipment by their employer, a practice that is now uncommon for the other categories of homeworkers. Similarly, the costs of electricity, heating, and broadband costs for contractually based homeworkers may be paid although they may incur tax liabilities for the employee.

## Technology

Technology and the digital workspace are clearly critical enablers for the adoption of agile working and require a number of pre-implementation activities to be undertaken.

### *Revision of IT and Security Policies*

There are a number of IT and security policies, as listed in Table 10.2, that should be reviewed as they may require amendment where more remote working is expected to be undertaken as a result of the adoption of agile working.

***Table 10.2 IT and security policies for review***

| | |
|---|---|
| Desktop/IT support and availability | Usage of the organization's equipment |
| Office services support, including postal arrangements | Use of employees' personal equipment |
| Computer security | Risk assessment |
| Data protection | Internet access |
| Document retention | Clean desk |

An important way of addressing the security risks of agile working is to ensure that employees are aware of their responsibilities. An acceptable use policy should clearly define the terms and conditions agile workers must agree to before they are allowed to connect devices to the corporate network. In reality, although some employees may not regard themselves as agile workers, their use of mobile technologies has afforded managers and employees the same benefits, and security risks, when traveling to, and attending, offsite meetings. Therefore the security policy should apply to all employees.

Homeworking poses additional security risks that need to be mitigated. While the use of virtual layering will enable employees to work securely at home using their personal computers, the homeworking policy should alert employees to privacy issues from other members of, or visitors to, the household having sight of confidential data. The use of a house telephone for work purposes is an obvious no-no where there is a risk of other members of the household taking calls.

An agile working policy should require agile workers who use mobile devices to install various security tools on them and change security configurations. However manually entering security configuration settings, and selecting patches, is highly subject to human error and in practice requires the oversight and assistance of the IT team.

In practice, organizations will have differing demands for security. Some such as those in the financial, or personal care, sectors will need very high-level security and control at all times, while others may require only moderate or low levels. A thorough risk assessment of serious security breaches with effective mitigation should be undertaken to determine that the policy is fit for purpose. However, be aware that a Vodafone survey found that 51 percent of employees admit they would ignore company policies that restrict the use of their own technology.[1]

### *Testing Infrastructure and Systems*

Effective and reliable IT and telephony systems (including videoconferencing) are key to the successful implementation of agile working. Agile workers will need to be confident that they will enjoy a robust and reliable IT service especially if there have been past issues with ICT provision. Connectivity is key to agile working, so the Wi-Fi coverage of all the organization's premises workspace should also be tested to ensure it is reliable and fit for purpose in terms of bandwidth and speed.

In addition to testing the robustness of the infrastructure the remote access to critical systems should be validated by systems testing and user acceptance testing involving agile workers to ensure they function correctly and at acceptable speeds. Employees will be reluctant to work away from their office base if the system performance is significantly inferior to that when used in the office environment. However, the increasing use of web-based systems is overcoming this issue.

---

[1] Vodafone proprietary research.

### *Extension of IT Support*

Agile workers will require extended IT support when issues arise when they are working in evenings and at weekends. There are a number of ways in which additional support could be resourced, for example, in-house, with IT employees themselves, adopting agile working to extend the hours they can offer or by the organization entering into a contract with a company to provide out-of-hours support.

### *Digitization*

An important aspect of agile working and the digital workspace is the ability to access all formats of information from a variety of locations—whether office-based, or working remotely, or at home. This capability is enhanced with the digitization of paper-based records. However, the scanning of paper documents is time-consuming and expensive and needs to be proportionate. Many paper documents will never be used again and have been kept "just in case." However, changes in data protection legislation mean that documents should be destroyed, rather than scanned if there is no legitimate need to keep them. Unnecessary digitization of paper documents will be costly and could cause a delay in the implementation of agile working. The scanning of documents that are required to be retained should be scheduled to meet the deadlines of agile working program plan.

### *Online Booking System*

The acquisition of an online booking system supported by booking protocols for shared resources, such as hotdesks and meeting rooms, will ensure that the availability of these facilities is known across the organization and that the facilities are used effectively.

## Facilities Package

To simplify deployment and delivery an identified package of standard facilities and technology (i.e., desk, physical storage and other space allocation, IT equipment) should be established for each workstyle identified from the workstyle analysis described in Chapter 7.

The business case may have been constructed on a standard agility ratio, for example, six desks for every 10 employees. However, in preparing for the implementation of agile working this approach may be too demanding in some teams and too generous in others. So an element of flexibility is likely to be needed at the time of implementation. Changes to the standard agility ratio should be justified by transparent business needs to avoid teams feeling that others have been more favorably treated.

Specific consideration should also be given to the sighting of work settings. Where agile workers with multi-site, or roaming workstyles, regularly work with teams with fixed desk, or fixed location, workstyles, additional desks, acting as touchdown spaces, should be made available immediately adjacent to the fixed desks. These facilities could also be used for visitors and members of partner organizations who also need to interact with fixed desk, or fixed location, employees.

In addition to the allocation of workstations, shared "alternative work settings" will be required to support various forms of activity-based working. In these communal areas, across each floor (usually close to major circulation routes such as meeting room areas, lobbies, and staircases) touchdown spaces could be provided to ensure that each hub office has sufficient space for the requirements of occupiers' workstyle. A variety of meeting areas and rooms should be located adjacent to touchdown areas. Some of these facilities should be unreserved, but the majority should be bookable through the online system.

## Learning

While directive training is the antithesis of agile working, which provides employees with choices in how they work, there will probably need to be some formal training for agile workers, for example, in the use of new technologies, legal, and security requirements. However, the crucial element is for managers and employees to understand the concept of agile working and develop ways in which it can be applied in practice that everyone can sign up to. This is where facilitated workshops are likely to prove useful.

The learning program should be part of the culture change program and should ensure that employees are equipped with the right skills and attitudes to practice agile working effectively. Induction learning for new joiners should be revised to include agile working.

An effective learning program will:

- Provide management and employees with the necessary knowledge, insight, and practical understanding of agile working.
- Encourage managers to challenge their own assumptions and beliefs and foster open-mindedness.
- Establish the new behaviors and protocols required for the new way of working.
- Set the rules, standards, and expectations in the way we work and behave in the workplace and the way we carry out an activity.

> *New ways of working will inevitably lead to gaps in skills and knowledge required for new ways of working. A learning needs analysis should be used to identify these shortcomings and to put plans in place to ensure that the right learning is obtained and provided.*

As there is likely to be a greater reliance on technology for communication, there should be positive examples to show how collaborative and communication technologies can compensate for the perceived advantages of traditional fixed office working.

### *Structuring the Learning Content*

A traditional approach to equip employees with the skills required for agile working is to provide separate learning experiences for managers and the broader workforce although elements will be common to both learning programs.

Managers will need to be briefed as to how to select the appropriate workstyles so that employees are allocated to an appropriate workstyle based on the requirements of their role.

Table 10.3 suggests the proposed contents of an agile working learning program for managers.

*Table 10.3 Proposed contents of an agile working learning program for managers*

| Modules | Topics |
|---|---|
| Managing remote and office teams together | • Managing different workstyles<br>• Personality and performance<br>• Managing by results<br>• Unconscious bias |
| Managing the transition to agile working | • Overcoming resistance to change<br>• Providing a role model<br>• Building trust |
| Using technology as a management tool | • Conference calls<br>• Sharing documents<br>• Monitoring and dashboard tools |
| Supporting employees | • Maintaining team spirit<br>• Identifying and addressing feelings of isolation and stress<br>• Proactive communication<br>• Feedback loops |

More senior managers may require a higher-level workshop based on business benefits and risks.

Table 10.4 suggests the proposed contents of an agile working learning program for employees.

*Table 10.4 Proposed contents of an agile working learning program for employees*

| Modules | Topics |
|---|---|
| Handling the transition | • Working without paper |
| Working at home | • Clarifying real and perceived limitations of homeworking<br>• Display screen equipment regulations<br>• Ergonomics (seating adjustment)<br>• Health and safety regulations<br>• Hints and tips—do's and don'ts |
| Working in shared workspaces | • Etiquette and team protocols |
| Security | • IT security and confidentiality in the office at home and other work locations |

| **Staying in touch** | • Informal knowledge sharing<br>• Maintaining local knowledge<br>• Developing effective "virtual" relationships<br>• Developing trust |
|---|---|
| **Digital ways of working** | • Conference calls<br>• Collaboration tools and alternatives to e-mail<br>• Working without paper |
| **Staying motivated** | • Dealing with the loss of "facetime"<br>• Workwrapping and managing your work–life balance<br>• Time management |

Another approach that can prove very effective is to base workshops on teams. We have found that facilitated workshops for managers and employees are an effective way to introduce the concept and address the practicalities. They provide the opportunity for concerns and issues to be raised and practical solutions to be proposed and agreed. While new joiners may have experience from their previous employment to contribute to a discussion of new ways of working, for many agile working will be a new concept. For this reason, it is preferable to involve an external facilitator who has extensive experience of the successful implementation of agile working.

Unlike more formal methods of training, workshops provide the opportunity for managers and their teams to internalize the new concepts and establish practical ways to implement new ways of working within their own team environments. Facilitated workshops also provide agile workers with the opportunity to recognize and appreciate workstyles that are different from their own.

## Establishing Work Etiquette and Protocols for Agile Working

A new smarter workplace requires consideration of changes in the way we behave and work. There are four levels of workplace behavioral guidance:

1. Corporate mandatory guidance and policies
2. Departmental guidance and policies

3. Team protocols and etiquettes
4. Individual behaviors for those employees who have special needs

These behaviors are more likely to be accepted and followed if they are discussed and explained in a workshop environment. New protocols will need to be encouraged and reinforced in the early stages of the implementation of new ways of working so that they become established practice. Some organizations rigorously enforce a clear desk policy removing items left on desks overnight, but this may antagonize employees. Analysis of room bookings and observation can be used to monitor behaviors. Table 10.5 suggests protocols and etiquette that should be considered.

*Table 10.5 Examples of work etiquette*

| | |
|---|---|
| **Sharing desk space** | |
| | • Should phone calls be taken at the desk?<br>• Should employees move to a meeting room for impromptu meetings and social conversations? |
| | • What food and drink can be consumed at a desk? (eating away from desks encourages social interaction) |
| | • Is there a clear desk policy, how will it be applied and enforced? |
| **Support spaces** | |
| | • Booking meeting spaces that are appropriate and the right size for the activity<br>• Canceling a booking as soon as a room is no longer required |
| | • Finishing on time, so the following meeting is not delayed |
| **Managing mobility** | |
| | • Considering team needs, as well as personal needs, when choosing to work away from an office base |
| | • Active calendar management, so colleagues know of your availability for phone calls and online discussion |
| | • Actively staying in touch with colleagues when away from the office |
| **Communication** | • Setting response times for replying to text messages, voicemails, and e-mails |
| | • Appropriate behaviors on conference calls and videoconferences |

## Providing Ongoing Support for Agile Working

There should be ongoing support to help managers and employees to embrace new ways of working. Therefore before the rollout of agile working, it is useful to set up a mechanism for ongoing support during the implementation. This support should be kept under continuous review and expanded as issues are addressed and lessons learned.

A branded portal for the agile working program could be set up. It could contain:

- User guides
- Relevant policies
- Work etiquette and protocols
- Floor plans
- Instructions on how to use the electronic booking system
- Access to learning materials
- Frequently asked questions (FAQs)
- Program communications and messages
- Helpline

## Rolling Out Agile Working

Once the preparatory activities are in place, the rollout of agile working to the functions of the organization in an agreed sequence can begin.

Then the following steps are suggested as part of this process:

1. In-scope teams will be identified ahead of the move into refreshed or new accommodation.
2. Local team or departmental agile working champions are identified and appointed.
3. Managers are briefed on the range of workstyles available and the anticipated relevance of the choices to the roles in their team(s). The options presented must be seen as applicable to all, subject only to clearly understandable and fair criteria (such as job role, performance, or personal circumstance). There should be communications about the process of applying and approving the choices made.

4. One-to-one discussions should be arranged with individual team members. The debate should take into account the role-based activities and team-related tasks. Where people have a choice in the way they work, there is a critical part to play in informing them of the appropriateness of those choices. Employees should have the opportunity to suggest ideas for working more efficiently with more autonomy. Managers and team members should discuss how changing ways of working could improve effectiveness, reduce travel, and improve productivity.

*A preferred workstyle may not be appropriate for roles where security risks prevent employees working away from the organization's premises.*

5. The agreed workstyle should be communicated to the:
   - **Facilities Department**—to enable allocation of appropriate desk and storage facilities according to the approved agility ratio.
   - **IT Department**—to agree, issue, and record a suitable technology package (computers and other devices, software tools, and authorized access).
   - **HR Department**—to record compliance, learning, and agreement of the chosen workstyle with an indication of the review period.
   - **Line Managers**—to validate records, confirm the outcome of discussions, and manage the individual's migration to agile working and specified workstyle.
6. On moving to new accommodation, teams would occupy spaces in accordance with the ratios previously defined, and a review of both accommodation and occupancy should be carried out approximately two months after the move.

Issues should be recorded as they occur and addressed as quickly as possible, so momentum is maintained. Any lessons learned after each rollout stage should be considered and acted upon before the next stage is implemented.

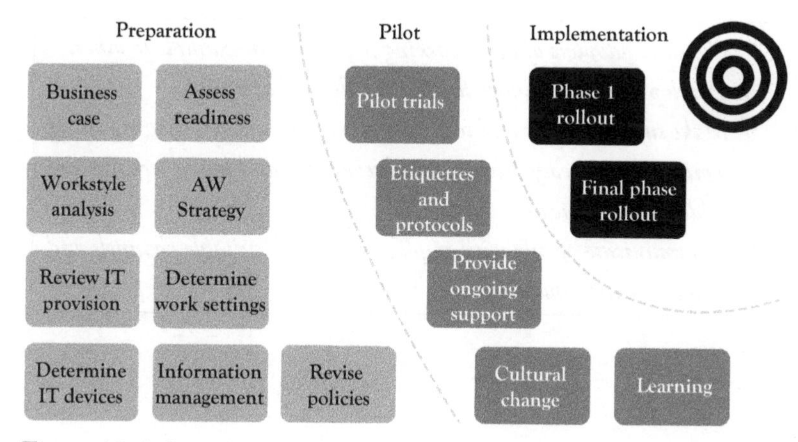


***Figure 10.1 Stepping stones in an agile working transformation map***

Figure 10.1 summarizes the activities described in Part III of this book into the preparation, pilots, and full implementation of the agile working program.

*Here's a 10-point plan to deliver agile working:*

1. *Develop a business case with clear business benefits and mechanisms to ensure they are realized.*
2. *Seek out a champion who advocates agile working and has the authority to ensure that sufficient resources are made available to the program.*
3. *Think through the risks of introducing agile working and develop some mitigating strategies.*
4. *Develop clear guidelines and objectives. Many organizations claim their employees have autonomy in their workstyle, but what is or isn't allowed is often determined by line managers and their attitudes. Clear guidelines will help to remove personal attitudes that frustrate agile working.*
5. *Test the approach by running a small-scale pilot scheme for a set time period. Gather feedback, evaluate it, and make the required changes.*
6. *Concentrate on quick wins, starting with departments who want to change, so objectives are more readily delivered.*

7. *Use early adopters of agile working to provide an example to others.*
8. *Develop managers' understanding, skills, and acceptance.*
9. *Make sure managers and teams have very focused targets so reporting against them is easy. Recognize achievements and make sure they are widely communicated.*
10. *Communicate openly with employees using all suitable channels and make sure the communication is two-way.*

# PART IV

# Sustaining and Progressing Agile Working

The final phase of an agile working program is the embedding of agile working and digital workspace practices into the accepted ways of working, sometimes called a business as usual model. What was initially new and a challenging form of working should become routine.

One of the ongoing challenges of agile working is the management of remote workers where employees are out of sight and may be working at different times than their manager is working. Managing remote workers can be done well if managers take the time to understand how to set up a supportive remote working environment that relies on trust, frequent communication, and an inclusive culture for those employees working remotely. While a small number of high-profile companies, such as Yahoo and IBM, have brought remote workers back into an office environment, remote working is now recognized as beneficial for the employer as well as the employee. As explained below not all employees will want to work remotely but the vast majority, especially among the later work generations, will seek and expect this option. And few organizations could afford the property costs incurred by reinstituting office accommodation.

Predicting the future is a challenging activity but the current consensus on the most significant technological developments that will contribute to new ways of working in the near future are artificial intelligence, the Internet of Things, and smart buildings.

# CHAPTER 11

# Managing Agile Workers

Agile working encourages individual initiative but within a teamworking approach. Agile working teams are often virtual teams with members working at different times and locations. The digital workspace enables team members to share information electronically, such as their work schedules and work-in-progress electronic documents that can be readily accessed by other team members.

The management of virtual teams is different from that of physically located teams and is often quite challenging. Agile workers need to be empowered to make their own decisions, within their level of competence and agreed parameters, so they can react quickly and appropriately regardless of where they are situated. Agile workers want clear objectives but will resist micromanagement.

Trust is a crucial component. There are many business benefits of adopting agile working but it will only happen if managers and employees feel they have the competence and confidence to accept this new way working. Managers need to trust agile workers and, in turn, agile workers need to demonstrate that they can be trusted. This trust is not unconditional; managers will need regular reports that progress is on track and to be alerted in time to be able to intervene if problems arise.

To gain the trust of their manager and colleagues, agile workers should aim to demonstrate commitment and motivation and build up a good track record in performing well as an agile worker.

## Skills Required of Managers of Agile Workers

Managers of agile workers need to have all the skills for agile working as well as the skills for managing agile workers.

### *Skills Required of Agile Workers*

Starting with attitudinal skills, agile workers need to demonstrate a willingness to take responsibility for what they do. The trade-off for gaining more autonomy in how an agile worker works is accepting greater responsibility in meeting work commitments. Agile workers will also need to show a readiness to change how they work and also be willing and able to suggest how they could do things differently to achieve a better outcome, that is, be a "self-starter" in "CV speak." It is the outcomes on which they will be judged rather than the time they spend doing a task. They will have to accept that they will not be praised just for putting in long hours or working hard. In many roles, agile workers need to be able to work collaboratively with colleagues with some give-and-take to assist them to meet their targets as well as their own.

Technology is an essential enabler of many agile working processes so agile workers will need to be comfortable and competent in using electronic devices that are necessary for their workstyle. They need to embrace their digital workspace. They will need to be confident and competent in using software applications, particularly in the use of collaboration tools.

In what is a far less structured environment than traditional office-based working, agile workers need to have excellent organizational skills and be good time managers. Good communication skills are also essential, especially when using electronic messaging, to share and obtain information from colleagues working at different locations.

### *Leadership Skills Required for Managing Agile Workers*

Managers need to adopt a management attitude that is appropriate for agile working. McGregor categorized managers as Theory X or Theory Y.[1]

A *Theory X* manager believes that people inherently dislike work and prefer to be directed and consequently must be coerced or controlled.

---

[1] McGregor, D.M. April 1957. "The Human Side of Enterprise" In *Adventure in Thought and Action*, Proceedings of the Fifth Anniversary Convocation of the School of Industrial Management. Cambridge, MA: Massachusetts Institute of Technology.

These managers can feel they are losing control if employees are not under their watchful eye. Such views are often found in newly appointed first-line managers who may have a fear of losing control. This attitude is clearly antithetic to agile working. A *Theory Y* manager believes that people view work as being as natural as play and rest, and learn to accept and seek responsibility. They think that only a light-touch management style is required, as employees will exercise self-direction and control. These managers give individuals responsibility and trust them to get on with the job. Theory Y managers have a much higher chance of successfully managing agile workers. It is difficult to measure the time that agile workers spend on tasks when they are not under the watchful eye of their manager but, even if this was possible to evaluate this input, it does not measure the quantity or quality of their output. With agile working, a management by results style explicitly based on objective measures of output and outcomes is an appropriate method of managing performance and productivity. This change may be difficult for employees, as well as managers, who have been used to being praised for the time that they have devoted to a task. To build esprit de corps, rewards and celebration of achievements should be based on the group rather than individuals' performance. For managers who have relied on face-to-face communications, videoconferencing technologies can enable managers to "see and hear" their employees and even observe their body language. Once trust is established communications via messaging will often be sufficient. But regular contact is essential if trust is to be maintained.

*In practice, agile working requires leadership rather than management. Leadership is the ability to influence change and not a question of position in a hierarchy. Leaders get involved personally and show sustained commitment over time.*

### Other Management Skills

Managers are responsible for meeting business goals and getting results. The organization of resources is often their direct responsibility and control remains with them. While agile working performance should be based on objective measures of output, managers need to allow flexibility in how these outputs are achieved. Managers will need to be competent in performance management and target setting. They should be able to evaluate success through what has been accomplished and, crucially, who has contributed to the achievements.

While communication is always an essential management skill, it becomes absolutely indispensable in a less structured environment when managers and employees are in different locations and personal "time zones." Managers will need to have strong communication skills so that the goals they set are clearly expressed to their team, and each member of the team understands their manager's expectations and objectives.

Managers should lead by example in using the tools of the digital workspace to communicate. Managers will need to become adept in the practical use of videoconferencing and teleconferencing technologies while still making some time available for regular face-to-face meetings. They need to be proficient in choosing the appropriate tools for different communication objectives, for example, to persuade, assess workloads, delegate, or inform. They should keep their electronic calendars up to date, so everyone knows when they are contactable.

Specific interpersonal skills good managers should possess will also be needed for managing agile workers. These include listening, influencing, and negotiation skills to obtain changes in employees' behaviors. Coaching skills are required to develop employees to accept alternative ways of working. Emotional intelligence, that is, awareness of the impact of their own actions on others, is an important attribute to acquire as a manager of agile workers.

## Managing Home Workers

Working at home creates challenges for employees and their managers. Employees can adopt different attitudes to homeworking, as described below, and managers will need empathy in managing employees working at home.

Some agile workers, **"the isolationists"** (see Figure 11.1), seek to cut themselves off from all distractions to focus on their specific tasks, such as writing a report. This inherently selfish attitude can be challenging to employees' colleagues, as they are unsure when the isolationists are

*Figure 11.1 The Isolationist*

available to be contacted and how promptly they will respond to requests. Managers should resist adopting this workstyle themselves as this sets a negative precedent. The isolationist should be encouraged to learn and apply sound diary management skills to indicate their availability and should be coached to work collaboratively.

**"The Time Shifter"** (see Figure 11.2) can also be a challenge. They choose to work at hours that suit their personal circumstances, such as caring responsibilities, and consequently are not available throughout the normal working day. The opportunities for audio conversations are therefore restricted, so good electronic communications and use of collaborative skills are essential for both management and employees.

Change is often resisted and despite training and support not all employees will be comfortable away from a traditional office routine where they have enjoyed the company and support of their colleagues. For **"The Reluctant Absentees"** (see Figure 11.3) a manager needs to employ counseling and negotiation skills to coax these employees into an agile working environment.

*Figure 11.2 The time shifter*

*Figure 11.3 The reluctant absentees*

Agile working, when mobile working and homeworking are the main workstyles, is often associated with lone(ly) working but this should not be the case. Agile working doesn't mean working without the support of colleagues. In some instances, agile working promotes more collaboration, with employees from across different departments working together to achieve a common goal. The improvement of collaborative technologies over the past few years has also made communication faster and easier than before.

**"The Remote Manager"** (see Figure 11.4) is the model that many agile working managers themselves aspire to, demonstrating that it is perfectly possible to manage remotely through their digital workspace and still be readily accessible to all members of their team.

*Figure 11.4 The remote manager*

Being sensitive to the needs of agile workers will overcome most of, if not all, the issues associated with agile working. Furthermore, many of these practices, such as focusing on outcomes, rather than the time spent by agile workers sitting at a computer, are good for managing all employees including those who remain office-bound. Clearly, managers cannot afford to treat one group of employees more favorably than another.

## How Personality Affects Agile Workers' Productivity

The author led a research study on the attitudes and performance of agile workers.[2] Most analyses of agile workers' requirements are based on workstyles related to job roles, for example, office-based working, homeworking, mobile working, and so on. However, the successful introduction of new ways of working relies on the willingness of the people occupying the job roles to embrace new ways of working—agile working needs to accommodate their personalities. There has been little investigation of the needs of agile workers with different personality types beyond looking at the needs of extroverts and introverts.

We undertook research that looked at the links between agile working, personality, and performance to see if different people are more suited to different ways of working and if organizations should use different approaches to agile working employees to increase their productivity. The research, carried out in the UK, was commissioned by the Employers Network for Equality & Inclusion (enei) with sponsorship from DWF, a major law firm, and Santander, an international bank. Employees and managers from Birmingham City Council, the Department for Work and Pensions, the Ministry of Justice, and the National Health Service (NHS) also participated in the survey, 584 in total. The research examined four main personality types based on the DiSC® profiling technique summarized in Figure 11.5. DiSC is a well-proven test used by some 41 million people across 50 countries since 1984.

### *Performance and Personality Profile*

Employees from different workstyles categories were asked to rate their performance across a range of performance measures. To check the validity of the employees' perceptions these employees' line managers were also asked to assess the performance of their employees. In general, line managers' responses validated their employees' responses.

---

[2] Eary, J. 2015. "Research report on Agile Working, Personality & Performance." JEC Professional Services and the Employers' Network for Equality and Inclusion.

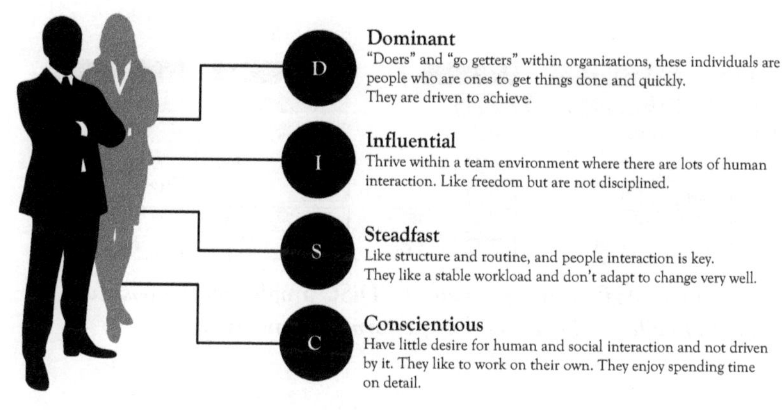


*Figure 11.5 The DiSC personality types*

The proportion of agile workers who were rated "exceptional" or "very good" varied according to their personality profile. The performance of the agile workers with a steadfast personality had the highest overall performance ratings, although agile workers with a dominant personality came out top for efficiency and productivity. The agile workers with an influential personality showed good performance, but of the four groups they appeared to find agile working most challenging.

### *Rating of Agile Working by Employees with Different Personality Types*

The agile workers' views on the positive impact of agile working on some performance measures were ascertained. In general, there were no significant differences between respondents based on age, gender, job role, length in job role, or employment status. When examined by personality profiles, effectiveness, responsiveness, responsibility, and job satisfaction all had similar scores. However, as Figure 11.6 shows, employees with an influential personality profile were less positive about agile working's contribution to efficiency, productivity, and quality of work than employees with other types of personality profiles while the views of employees with dominant, steadfast, and conscientious personality were broadly similar.

Ratings varied according to personality type for a number of other factors as shown in Figure 11.7. While all participants valued reliable technology, there was little interest in more sophisticated technology

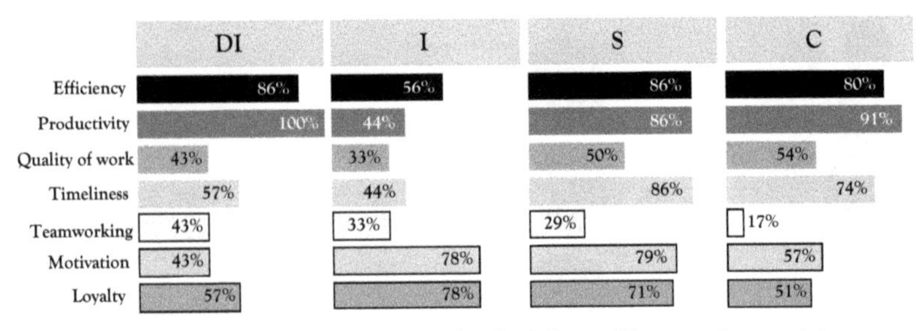


***Figure 11.6 Agile workers' views by DiSC profiles on the positive impact of agile working on other performance measures***

tools. Surprisingly, good workplace facilities were rated as "very important" by less than 40 percent of respondents and particularly low by those employees with a dominant personality, possibly reflecting the amount of work that now takes place away from an office.

| | DI | I | S | C |
|---|---|---|---|---|
| Interaction with manager | 14% | 56% | 21% | 37% |
| Interaction with colleagues | 57% | 67% | 57% | 54% |
| Calendar/diary management | 57% | 78% | 86% | 74% |
| Good workplace facilities | 14% | 22% | 36% | 37% |
| Opportunities to be creative | 71% | 89% | 50% | 43% |

***Figure 11.7 Factors rated as "very important" for achieving good performance by different personality types***

Those with an influential personality profile appeared to have the most challenges, particularly with teamworking, although this was also an issue across a number of personality types. Teamworking was the only example of agile working having a negative impact on performance. Overall, less than a third of agile workers felt that their way of working had a positive effect on teamworking with some believing that it had an adverse effect. Furthermore, 20 percent of employees with a conscientious personality felt that agile working had a negative impact on teamworking, more than those with a positive view. A third of respondents with an influential personality held a negative view, but this was matched with those who had a positive view. Teamworking is an important factor in performance although it is difficult to get right. From the survey responses, it appears that the implementation of agile working and the digital workspace in a number of the participating organizations has not effectively addressed teamworking. The survey suggested that the survey respondents did not regard social events and social media, or at least the way they were being run, as relevant.

### *Managing Agile Workers with Different Personality Types*

We concluded that employees need to be managed in different ways:

- **"Dominant employees"** are most likely to enjoy the control available to them through agile working, and will be focused, needing minimal supervision or interaction. Managers provide an element of structure and objectives to be achieved. They should contact the employees regularly to ensure that they are not departing from set objectives.
- **"Influential employees"** will require active management through direction, expectation setting, and opportunities to communicate with the broader team and may need more regular communication than others. Managers should schedule contact calls at the start and end of each day and encourage these employees to use conferencing facilities.
- **"Steadfast employees"** may find agile working harder to adapt to and are more likely to work nine to five anyway. Managers should make regular contact and set a clear structure including daily or weekly targets for deliverables. Managers should demonstrate their trust in these employees and make them feel at ease in their new working environment.
- **"Conscientious employees"** are likely to thrive in an agile working environment without distractions, but require supervision to ensure that they do not work excessive hours and burn out. Managers should encourage interaction with themselves and other team members through the use of conference calls and other communication mechanisms.

Clearly, a "one size fits all" approach is unlikely to succeed. The conclusion is that the key to obtaining good performance from adopting agile working is to recognize the needs of employees with different personality profiles.

Organizations also need to focus on of the factors that contribute to effective performance for agile working for all employees, specifically communication, effective teamwork, and diary management to overcome the lack of face-to-face interaction between agile workers, their colleagues, and their line managers. The provision of an appropriate, reliable technology is important, as are fast reliable networks, good remote access to data, and application systems that work well when used remotely.

Our research showed that there are clear business benefits from organizations adopting agile working and the performance benefits are likely to be greater when employees are involved in its implementation. The lack of face-to-face interaction between agile workers, their colleagues, and their line managers can be overcome through the use of effective communications and conferencing facilities, and through managed learning. The research found that if managers are not good role models or fail to be ambassadors for agile working its implementation has less chance of sustained success.

# CHAPTER 12

# Continuing the Agile Working Journey

The new way of working should be fully sustainable as technology and facilities evolve, and people are recruited or move on. Within an organization, some employees are likely to rotate through a number of different roles as their career develops and they may be assigned different workstyles that reflect their new positions.

Of course, this does not mean that the practices associated with what were new ways of working are frozen forever. Organizations should adopt a policy of continuous improvement. In many ways, agile working can be regarded as a journey, but the essential philosophy/concept of employee autonomy within necessary constraints should endure.

## Sustaining Agile Working

There should be continuing investment in people, technology, and workspaces to support evolving ways of working. The critical elements of the agile working strategy should be reviewed such as workstyles, policies, and protocols to ensure their relevance and currency to changing situations.

### *Monitoring*

The new processes should continue to be monitored to ensure employees are not drifting back to former ways of working. For example, some employees may resort to sitting at the same shared desk so that over time they regard it as their own.

As agile working is embedded within an organization, it is not unusual to see changing patterns of working create different space utilization from that originally planned. It is, therefore, best practice to build in regular reviews and surveys of office space utilization that may lead to further opportunities for space rationalization. This reduction in the space required may lead to a reappraisal of the estate strategy.

Similarly with the digital workspace organizations should maintain a commitment to regularly review, gather user feedback, and refresh the platform in line with business and user needs.

### *Measures to Reinforce Agile Working*

There are a number of actions that can be taken to strengthen and enhance agile working.

- Maintain agile working as the preferred way of working.
- Continue to drive culture change from top to bottom.
- Establish role models and "tell stories" that reinforce desired behaviors and the new culture.
- Embed agility working into job design at all levels.
- Create metrics that indicate and track the progress of the agile working journey.
- Communicate and celebrate success in the adoption of agile working both by the organization and by the individuals.

### *Addressing Persistent Issues*

Given a choice, many employees would prefer not to be in their office base, on Mondays and Fridays. These preferences can lead to an uneven use of facilities, for example, meeting rooms are underutilized on these days but oversubscribed on Tuesdays, Wednesdays, and Thursdays. More serious is when employees' lack of availability affects customer service or operational delivery. Employees should be made aware that their availability should match the predicted demand. Ideally, this can be resolved by discussion and agreement within the team but may require management directive to ensure services are not impacted.

## How Agile Workers Will Work in the Future

Arguably the most significant technological developments that will impact agile working in the near future are artificial intelligence, the Internet of Things, and smart buildings.

### *Artificial Intelligence*

Artificial intelligence (AI) has moved from a topic of academic research to mainstream business tool. Gartner[1] predicts that AI will be the most disruptive class of technologies for the next decade. In a survey of IT decision makers that my company, CCS Insight,[2] conducted in July 2017, 58 percent of respondents said that they are using, testing, or researching the use of AI in their organizations. Repetitive processes can be automated with robotics and AI. McKinsey & Company[3] believes that every occupation has at least partial automation potential and estimates that half of all current employees' activities could be automated by adapting recently demonstrated technologies. However, an automated workforce is unlikely to eliminate people from the workplace, but the work they do will be redefined. Humans will focus more on creativity to develop better solutions.

AI presents exciting opportunities to advance productivity in the intelligent digital workplace, and here are some examples:

- **Productivity apps**. These are able to automate tasks that are simple but can be time-consuming. Assistive cognitive features improve the performance of search tools, enabling quicker access to documents, support automated e-mail replies, and power virtual assistants that can display contextually relevant information for users. The next generation of workplace sensors can link the use of physical space to business performance. A research project at the University of Cambridge has used radio-frequency identification (RFID) tags that detect face-to-face interactions to understand how interaction is influenced by spaces provided in the workplace.[4]

---

[1] Cearley, D.W., B. Burke, S. Searle, and M.J. Walker. October 2017. "Top 10 Strategic Technology Trends for 2018." *Gartner.*

[2] "Security, AI and Microsoft Are Shaping the Digital Workplace. 2017." CCS Insight's IT Buyer Survey.

[3] "A Future That Works: Automation, Employment, and Productivity. January 2017." McKinsey Global Institute.

[4] Brown, C., C. Efstratiou, I. Leontiadis, D. Quercia, C. Mascolo, J. Scott, and P. Key. 2014. "The Architecture of Innovation: Tracking Face-to-Face Interactions with ubicomp Technologies." Proceedings of the ACM International Joint Conference on Pervasive and Ubiquitous Computing.

Humanyze merges data from sociometric digital badges worn by employees with their calendars and e-mails to establish whether office layouts favor teamwork.

- **Voice control**. The integration of voice or natural language processing will further boost productivity. Employees will be able to create and complete documents using speech dictation or use natural language queries to parse data or control functions in spreadsheets.
- **Cybersecurity**. AI will be able to protect organizations' information and systems from spam, phishing attacks, and malware. Respondents to the 2017 survey of IT decision makers[5] listed cybersecurity as the most likely use of AI in their organizations.
- **Telepresence**. Robots will enable employees to work from any location across the world while also being virtually active in their company's home base. The use of holograms in the workplace will become more prevalent. A realistic 3D image appearing in the employee's home or working environment will remove the need for their physical presence in meetings.

Even with its increasing popularity, some organizations are hesitant to adopt even relatively simple AI features such as chatbots. There should be a trade-off between privacy and productivity. Employees should be told about the AI technologies that are being used in their workplace and what data is being gathered.

### *Internet of Things and Smart Buildings*

The Internet of Things (IoT) is the term used to describe a world in which devices are sensor-enabled, connected, and able to share information about their current state and environment over the Internet. Gartner[6]

[5] "Security, AI and Microsoft Are Shaping the Digital Workplace. 2017." CCS Insight's IT Buyer Survey.

[6] Gartner says 6.4 billion connected "Things" will be in use in 2016. Gartner, Business at Gartner Symposium/ITxpo 2015.

estimates that, by 2020, there will be 21 billion connected IoT devices (there were 900 million in 2009).

The installation of connected devices in buildings is one of the critical applications of IoT technology. The office buildings of the near future will have hundreds of thousands of sensors installed, monitoring everything from the performance of individual light settings to the health and well-being of employees.

Growing volumes of data from IoT sensors and developments in computing power will further transform building operations. Specialist neural software can analyze data from building sensors and combine this with external data, to predict the number of users that will be present in a building on a given day, and optimize services accordingly.

Buildings could contain virtual concierges that use natural language processing so that employees could interact with them, as with Apple's Siri or Amazon's Alexa. Virtual concierges could be used to control the working environment, book meeting rooms, and help track down colleagues.

Smart buildings are structures that harness smart technology, including IoT and machine learning. A smart building is aware of the employee's presence and shapes itself to their preferences. Smart buildings are also able to develop and adapt so that their solution is always relevant to their inhabitants. There are significant benefits to working in smart buildings including:

- Increased productivity by providing a better working experience through changing the environment to the employee's preferences.
- Improved well-being, for example, the employee's temperature and lighting settings automatically adjust to the employee's desired level as they move through the building.
- Enhanced security as facial recognition technology means employees do not have to use entry cards to access the building.
- Providing a dynamic work environment by enabling spaces to be easily reconfigured.
- Alerting employees to the location of colleagues with whom they are collaborating.

## A Glimpse at the World of Work in 2025

*An agile worker looks back at the many changes in the world of work.*

*At long last, we have at last got rid of the 20th-century working practices.*

*Nearly all my work activities are home-based now. My only business travel is a once a week trip to my local work hub if you can call a brisk walk, travel. It's an excellent opportunity to get out of the house and meet up with colleagues, and people I have got to know from other organizations, and exchange ideas, very stimulating!*

*It's been months since I needed to visit the company HQ and it's a much smaller building than it used to be. It's more like a hotel these days with comfy chairs and all sorts of rooms for different activities. There is even sleep pod where you can take a nap. They got rid of the last desks a few years ago. Remember all that fuss at the beginning of the century about "hotdesking" and how people were reluctant to share their desks. Why would you need a desk? If I want to see anything I can project it on to a wall or pop on my virtual reality glasses. Keyboards became redundant when artificial intelligence made speech recognition so accurate. Even the mouse has been discarded and now we can control our devices through gestures and voice commands.*

*There was that property crash a few years back when it was realized that we had far more office accommodation than office workers. A lot of offices have already been converted into housing or combined live/work dwellings. I can see offices disappearing altogether before too long. These immersive collaboration technologies, such as 3D videoconferencing and life-size holograms, are brilliant.*

*It's like being in the same room with people who might, in reality, be hundreds, or thousands, of miles away. We used to talk about the importance of a physical face-to-face meeting to meet people for the first time; well you can now do that in the comfort of your own home. They are even talking about links to our nervous systems to enable us to have a realistic virtual handshake.*

*So there is little need to travel. Do you remember the dreaded rush hour commuting with regular morning and evening traffic jams and people packed like sardines on trains? Of course, that's all gone now that the majority of employees are now home-based workers. At last, all this reduced travel has dramatically cut our carbon emissions. Even better these spray-on solar cells help reduce our energy bills as well helping the environment. They even work indoors, amazing!*

*Short-term and zero-hours contracts are now the norm. No one seems to have a full-time permanent job these days. Most people have a portfolio of jobs, usually part-time. But it can be tough. In my field, I am competing with people in China and India—with all the developments in video and virtual communications distance is no object.*

*While offices have got smaller, houses have got bigger. It seems all new builds have a built-in workspace so that all sorts of work activities can be done at home including small-scale manufacturing with 3D printers. Of course, it is essential to have a separate entrance to our family home for business visitors and deliveries.*

*A long-cherished dream of many of my friends, to be able to work in remote areas in the countryside, is now possible. With 6G networks with hyper-fast reliable broadband, people can work anywhere. Although home-based working has reduced the price pressures on the London housing market, it has pushed up the price of accommodation in the beauty spots in the Lake District and Cornwall. If only I had bought that cottage when I could have afforded it.*

*Home-based working has improved the quality of life of many of us. We used to talk about work–life balance, but the realities of instant and continuous communications mean that work and social life have become intertwined. It's all about work–life integration; you just need to manage your life sensibly. There are plenty of digital tools to help you. I can't imagine how we managed without our robot, Robbie, to keep the house clean and do other chores around the house. He even makes a decent cup of tea!*

# APPENDIX A
# Glossary

## Agile Working

"Bringing people, processes, connectivity and technology, time and place together to find the most appropriate and effective way of working to carry out a particular task. It is working within the guidelines (of the task) but without boundaries (of how you achieve it)."[1] Unlike flexible working, which is mainly regarded as providing employee benefits, agile working is regarded as offering business benefits as well as employee benefits.

## Agility Ratio

The number of people allocated to the number of desks (or how many desks are required to accommodate a given number of people). It is usually expressed as the number of people assigned to 10 desks.

## Business Transformation

Business transformation is a somewhat overused term to describe fundamental changes in the business processes and technologies an organization employs to address a significant shift in the market or meet redefined business goals.

## BYOD

BYOD (Bring Your Own Device) refers to the policy of permitting employees to bring personally owned mobile devices (laptops, tablets, and smartphones) for work purposes. By keeping personal and business

---

[1] http://agile.org.uk/what-is-agile-working/

information on the same device many people are now practicing work–life integration, reducing the separation of time assigned for business and personal activities.

## Collaborative Tools

Collaborative working technologies enable people in different physical locations to work together, for example, by holding meetings or amending documents. There are asynchronous collaboration tools, such as e-mail, that enable people to communicate at a different time from each other. Synchronous collaboration tools, such as videoconferencing and instant messaging, enable people to work together at the same time.

## Digital Workplace

The digital workplace can be regarded as an extension of the physical workplace that includes the virtual environment as well as the physical workplace. Gartner describes it as: "The digital workplace enables new, more effective ways of working; raises employee engagement and agility; and exploits consumer-oriented styles and technologies."[2]

## Digital Workspace

It could be regarded as a synonym of the digital **workplace**. "It is the specific digital resources a person can access at any given time comprise their digital workspace. Ideally, this digital workspace will include all the resources they need to get their work done."[3]

Or more concisely, a digital workspace contains all the applications and data people require to work, accessible from any device.[4]

[2] https://gartner.com/it-glossary/digital-workplace

[3] http://www3.ressoftware.com/rs/794-EGN-208/images/What%20 ispercent20a %20Digital %20Workspace.pdf

[4] https://citrix.com/blogs/2016/03/14/5-reasons-enterprises-are-moving-to-digital-workspace-delivery/

## Dynamic Working

A synonym for agile working that is only used by a few organizations.

## Flexible Working

Flexible working is a general term for working at times and places away from the traditional full-time nine-to-five office-based employment. The definition on the gov.uk site[5] is skewed in favor of employees: "Flexible working is a way of working that suits an employee's needs, for example, being able to work certain hours or work from home." The examples given and defined on the site are job sharing, working from home, part-time working, compressed hours, flexitime, and annualized hours and staggered hours.

## Homeworking

Homeworking is a workstyle where some official work is done at home. There is an essential difference between those who are contractually based homeworkers, that is, their home is their designated place of work and they only visit their employer's premises for specific business reasons, and all other employees who work at home on occasions but who have a designated office as their place of work.

## Hotdesking

Hotdesking is a colloquial term to describe desks that are shared by employees at different times. It breaks the link between employees and designated desks and therefore increases the flexibility of accommodation and can result in cost savings from a reduction in the size of office accommodation.

---

[5] https://gov.uk/flexible-working

## The Internet of Things

The interconnection, via the Internet, of computing devices embedded in everyday objects, enabling them to send and receive data. These devices can communicate within a network, independently of human action.

## Mobile Working

Mobile working is a peripatetic workstyle, working "in the field" or out and about as in the old Martini slogan "anytime, anyplace anywhere," typically practiced by service engineers and sales employees.

## New Ways of Working

New ways of working is an umbrella term that embraces all alternative ways of working to the traditional full-time nine-to-five single office-based employment.

## Remote Working

Remote working describes working at bases away from a designated place of work, similar to mobile workers but limited to a few locations, and thus does not require mobile technologies to accomplish work tasks.

## Smart Working

A synonym for agile working, which has generally superseded it. However, the UK Civil Service deliberately use the term "smart working" to differentiate it from agile software development.

## Work–Life Balance

The concept of work–life balance sets boundaries between "worktime," that is, activities undertaken for your employer, and "non-worktime" for personal and social activities. Work–life balance is perceived as an employment benefit. Many employees are anxious that work requirements will not encroach on their personal time.

## Work–Life Integration

Work–life integration is a concept linked to agile working. It is the result of people deliberately mixing business and personal information on their devices in what is often called a connected lifestyle. As a consequence the separation between the time they spend on work and nonwork activities is blurred. It has encountered resistance from some employees who regard it as an intrusion into their personal life as they believe they are always available to their employers and find it difficult to stop thinking about work. Others see benefits in being able to switch flexibly between work and nonwork activities (see workwrapping).

## Workwrapping

Workwrapping is an approach adopted by employees who dynamically allocate their available time between work and nonwork activities. By focusing on clearly defined outputs employees can become more productive while prioritizing their time for social and family activities.

# About the Author

**John Eary** is a senior management consultant who has managed major assignments for the private, public, and not-for-profit sectors in Africa, Asia, and Europe. John has advised over 40 organizations in new ways of working. Recent assignments he has led include the assessment of agile working readiness and the development of an agile working strategy for a UK police force, the preparation of an extensive business case for an international bank, and research into agile working, personality, and performance. John writes a regular blog on agile working and frequently participates in seminars and webinars on the subject. He is a guest lecturer at the Royal Holloway College, University of London. Prior to establishing his own consultancy business in 2010. John was a senior consultant at NCC Group and was formerly Training and Multimedia Services Manager at the National Computing Centre. John has a Masters degree from Warwick University Business School. He regards himself as an Agile Worker and actively practices work-life integration and workwrapping.

# Index

## OTHER TITLES IN OUR PORTFOLIO AND PROJECT MANAGEMENT COLLECTION

Timothy J. Kloppenborg, Editor

- *Project Management and Leadership Challenges, Volume I: Applying Project Management Principles for Organizational Transformation* by M. Aslam Mirza
- *Innoliteracy: From Design Thinking to Tangible Change* by Steinar Valade-Amland
- *Project Management and Leadership Challenges, Volume II: Understanding Human Factors And Workplace Environment* by M. Aslam Mirza
- *Project Management and Leadership Challenges, Volume III: Respecting Diversity, Building Team Meaningfulness, and Growing Into Leadership Roles* by M. Aslam Mirza
- *Why Projects Fail: Nine Laws for Success* by Tony Martyr
- *Scrum for Teams: A Guide by Practical Example* by Dion Nicolaas
- *Project Management and Leadership Challenges, Volume IV: Agility in Project Management and Collaboration* by M. Aslam Mirza

Lightning Source UK Ltd.
Milton Keynes UK
UKHW022028070222
398329UK00009B/1842

9 781947 441538